Above: Michael Gerber's interview

Below: Joe Garner's interview

Skip a Step

Cover Design by Matthew Vasquez

Edited by Blake Pinto

Contributions by Debbie Powers

ISBN 978-1-64516-780-8

Copyright © 2019

Published by Happy Lifestyle Online

SkipAStep.net

LisaCaprelli.com

Huntington Beach, CA USA

Introduction

Journal to Accompany

Skip a Step: Imparting

Wisdom For Young

Entrepreneur Minds

Table of Contents

Introduction

So many young people are programmed from an early age to go to school, get good grades, attend college, and then hope for a good-paying job. This used to be the "safe" approach to obtaining a successful life. But every once in a while, a maverick comes along and bucks the trend. This person doesn't play it safe. Instead, they take risks. They put their heart and soul into building a company that has never existed before, offering a crucial product or service that no one else is providing. By doing something so disruptive and wholly original, they attain success on their terms. As a culture, we celebrate these gutsy individualists as entrepreneurs.

As we have dug deep into the radical minds of these entrepreneurs – we can understand what they value. In a sense, it is like receiving the secrets of life from iconoclasts discontented with the status quo. You may receive a wealth of knowledge, not only about bootstrapping a company from nothing—you may discover what it truly means to be a leader in an age in which conformity is emphasized and risk is carefully avoided.

But there's something more important that entrepreneurs can teach our young; something more vital than positive cash flow. These courageous men and women can offer the new generation a bounty of insight into what makes for a meaningful life. An entrepreneur's hard-won victories contain the full human drama: adversity, conflict, struggle, triumph, failure, and redemption. Scholar Joseph Campbell once put forth a theory that there is but one great story told in an infinite number of ways. He called it the "Hero's Journey" and it always involves one man or woman facing down the abyss alone through the sheer force of their will and their inability to give up despite all odds. At the end of the Hero's Journey, the individual always returns to his/her community with an elixir or wisdom to help others. Might we think of our entrepreneurs as these kinds of heroes, people who can illuminate unseen paths to brighten our lives?

Create the highest, GRANDEST vision for your life, because you BECOME what you believe!" - Oprah Winfrey

---

This book (the first in its series) is not another get rich quick guide from business moguls who amassed a fortune. It's meant for a new generation who doesn't just want to get rich, but wishes instead to find meaning and purpose in life. Each chapter contains a close interview with an entrepreneur divulging the wisdom they received from slaying the dragons in their own lives to achieve success. It is not just about wealth or success that we want you, the reader to walk away learning, but rather the struggle, triumphs and challenges others have faced.

It is important to know our transparent purpose is to pull at the heartstrings of you, our reader. We wish to challenge not only your minds, but your hearts, as to what is possible. We hope for you to learn that a successful life is a meaningful life and that each of us has something special to contribute if we face our challenges with courage, love and passion.

Dedications

By Lisa Caprelli:

This book would not be possible without the talent and collaboration of my co-author Michael Ashley. It took incredible vision, planning, execution and about 30 months to get this work into publication. Special thanks to Blake Pinto and son Matthew and sister Debbie and Ruth for your support with all the creative ideas I have! Thanks to each person and their voice in this book: Michael Gerber, Mitch Free, Dean Del Sesto, Joe Garner, Ted McGrath, Jim Fitzpatrick, Mark Shockley, Ken Kerry, Adryenn Ashley, Michael Reddick, Jessica Jackley. I acknowledge my family: Mamma Hope, Tia Lucy, Grandma and Grandpa, Matthew Vasquez, Trey Solomon, Mike Hernandez, Debbie Powers, Suzanne Funk, Ruth Leigh, Alyssa, Amanda, Andrew, Brandyn, Jasmine, and last but not least my loving man, Chris Herzig. Thank you for believing in me. Thanks to Keyana Martinez for helping me with the journal that accompanies this book and for understanding its vision!

By Michael Ashley:

This book is dedicated with love to my two boys: Teddy and Sammy. May you always follow your bliss and make the world a better place than you found it.

Chapter 1

"What If We Could?"

An interview with Michael Gerber, Business Guru and Author of the "E-Myth" Series

Michael's life of permanent searching

I was born into a Jewish Family in 1936, just preceding World War II and the Holocaust. As you can imagine, this wasn't the easiest time to be a Jew. Then again, there hasn't ever really been a great time to be a Jew. Throughout our history, we've been kicked out of countries and forced to survive. Our continuous exodus has made the Jewish people into grand assimilators.

Michael Gerber   1

I grew up during violent times and it was pretty much the end of my Judaism, along with most other Jews. Discarding my faith also ensured I grew up to be one of those grand assimilators, and I spent my life looking for meaning to seemingly fill in that void. Whether it was my constant questions, or studies of sales, philosophy, poetry, music, people, or even myself, my perpetual search was always to find meaning in life. Something deeper.

> My perpetual search was always to find meaning in life.

The 'Aha!' moment

I'm what you would refer to as a bit of a late bloomer. I was 38, heavily bearded, and a bit of an odd Jew when I picked up a hammer for the first time in my life. I had decided to become the apprentice of a true master carpenter so I could frame expensive homes. Somehow, I had this romantic notion of living off what I made with my hands, rather than talking and selling.

So there I was. 38 years old, following my mentor around, working an apprenticeship that most would have done at 16 years of age. I envisioned becoming a successful framing contractor up in Mendocino County. I'd be able to buy goats, chickens, horses, and of course, all the dope I could smoke; anything I wanted, really. I was just doing what I could to look after myself.

Fast-forward two years' time. I was up in Northern California visiting my sister and brother-in-law, Ace. Ace created advertising for high-tech startups in Silicon Valley with his company, Canadian Forum. Strangely enough, Ace had revealed to me in the past that I inspired him to go into business for himself.

This perceived business-savvy Ace saw in me must have influenced his next request because during my visit Ace asked if I would meet with one of his clients who was experiencing difficulty converting leads to sales. Shocked, I remember telling Ace I didn't know anything about his business or the technology industry.

"Don't worry," Ace assured me. "You know more than you think you do."

Ace introduced me to his client, Bob. Just as quickly as the stage was set, Ace left me alone with Bob, promising to return in an hour. Bob sized me up right away and asked, "What do you know about my product and business?"

"Nothing," I answered honestly.

Bob was floored. "If you don't know anything about my product or business then why are you here?"

I may not have known these things but I was determined to find them out. I spent the next hour bombarding Bob with questions so I could understand his business and his specific problems. Bob didn't have the answers to my questions and instead spoke in anecdotes. It quickly became apparent to me that the two assumptions I held entering this scenario were false.

First, Ace was right. I did know something about business. I knew that selling was a system. Secondly, my assumption that Bob knew how to operate a business simply because he owned a business was shattered.

I told Bob the solution to his problems was to implement a selling system to transform his current experience.

Bob liked that suggestion. "Can you create that for me?" he asked.

"Of course," I said.

This was the beginning of my entrepreneurship.

> *I told Bob the solution to his problems was to implement a selling system to transform his current experience...this was the beginning of my entrepreneurship.*

Even mistakes lead to opportunity

At the same time, Ace was busy at work, creating leads for his other clients. However, none of these businesses had any idea how they could convert such leads into billable customers. I saw an opening to capitalize my skills with Ace's clients, and began my business consultancy journey.

By the way, I hadn't yet learned my next brutal lesson and made the mistake of working for Ace's company directly. Never mix family and business! An enormous rift occurred between us and just like that, Ace found someone to replace me. His name was Tom. I could see why Ace chose him. Tom was a brilliant man with a background in the franchising industry.

When I was first introduced to Tom, he flat-out asked me what it is I do. I ended up spending the next couple of weeks with Tom, showing him the ins and outs of my approach. Tom came to me soon after with a proposition to start a business together, as opposed to working with Ace. That's how I started our business development firm, The Michael Thomas Corporation.

We were diving head first into uncharted waters. Our new endeavor was the first business coaching company ever created. Our dream was to transform the state of small business, advising them how they could expand worldwide.

Feeling the shakes

Every entrepreneur makes a conscious decision to pursue his or her dream. I like to refer to that inspirational drive as the 'entrepreneurial seizure'. It comes with the understanding an entrepreneur is completely dependent on creating work for his or herself. Part of the journey is feverishly working to accomplish what needs to be done without necessarily knowing how to do it. Entrepreneurship is a learning experience that often results in failure. Everyone has to struggle with moving through the process while learning what he or she doesn't yet understand.

It's important to know, however, my entrepreneurial seizure has never been driven by an interest in business. My motivation stems from my desire to create! This mindset has transformed me from what I would consider a simple technician into being a true entrepreneur, trying to determine how and why entrepreneurs approach a business task at hand.

The distinctive roles we play in our business

There are three different yet equally vital roles within a business: the entrepreneur, the technician, and the manager.

In my experience, this has evolved and taken new form. I have created a persona with very specific personality traits any true entrepreneurial leader should possess. These include the dreamer, thinker, storyteller, and leader. All four of these are absolutely necessary when developing a business. The dreamer begins with the dream, the thinker has the vision, the storyteller has the purpose, and the leader has a mission.

Your vision is fueled by your dream. My vision was to invent the McDonalds of small business consulting. In order to achieve this objective, my methods needed to be low cost, scalable, and replicable. My system also needed to be duplicable, just like the 37,000 locations across the globe comprising the McDonalds franchise. The purpose of my company was to enable every independently owned business to be as successful as the McDonalds franchise by following and utilizing a system. Of course, this was a ridiculously high bar my company set out to achieve. Few businesses are successful on their own, let alone held to the same standard of success as McDonalds.

"So what is your McDonalds?"

I'm always greeted by a strange look when I ask my clients this simple question. Their answer typically consists of their struggles demonstrating a lack of experience. This highlights the reality that most business owners don't know how to truly run a business because they aren't utilizing a system. It comes though real-world experience and trying to figure it out as you go.

Entrepreneurs need to approach business pragmatically, not academically. Don't be afraid to get your hands dirty and take your fair share of lickings. If you're given an answer that doesn't work, you need to ask more questions!

Discover what is missing from the picture so you can determine what needs to be done.

The four steps in the evolution of any successful enterprise

My experience helping entrepreneurs has revealed a common mistake made in the first few years of business. It's the misunderstanding of what a business really is. There are four important steps in the evolution of an enterprise.

The first step is the job. Second, there's practice. The third step is the business, which is ultimately followed by the enterprise. It's important to understand that an entrepreneur doesn't have a business until they've reached the third step.

The first step for anyone who aspires to create a great company is the job of creating a formal system to follow. Without a system in place, a business is doomed to failure. My job, or first step, was creating the Michael Thomas Business Development Program that we sold to small business owners.

It's imperative an entrepreneur invests the necessary time to practice the formal system of the product or service he or she has in place.

You don't have a replicable business you can sell if the core formal system isn't documented, organized, and systematized. My practice step consisted of generating leads, converting those leads to clients and then replicating our success for those clients.

Michael Gerber   7

Our system needed a process that could be followed and duplicated.

That was the most important and critical step of transforming my reality into becoming the McDonalds of small business consulting. It's a daunting amount of work to accomplish in the beginning. Perseverance and the entrepreneurial shake, however, will propel aspiring business owners through this task.

Eight turn-key practices you need to know

Building a business is simple. It's just a matter of putting the pieces together, like building with Lego blocks as a kid. A business has been established once a turnkey system has been developed that can be replicated. Simply put, a business is nothing more the following 8 turn-key practices.

1. Your dream.
2. Your vision.
3. Your purpose.
4. Your mission.
5. Your job.
6. Your practice.
7. Your business.
8. Your enterprise.

The beauty of this system is that anybody can follow these steps. It took me 80 years and a number of speed bumps along the path to understand business to the extent where it can all be reduced to these eight simple steps.

Pushing past other's expectations

I awoke from my slumber one day with an unfamiliar word lingering in my head from the remnants of a dream. The word 'Octogenarian' was seared into my mind. I decided to do some investigating and was shocked to discover it defines a person who is aged between 80-89 years old.

"Holy shit," I thought to myself. "What does this mean?"

This revelation helped explain why people always shoot me such odd glances. Here I am, an 80-year-old man working towards the impossible in developing business with the energy level and ambition of someone half my age.

The world judges me by my appearance. Their expectation is I should be retired, sitting around somewhere. Learning what an Octogenarian was gave me a sense of self-awareness I didn't even have when I first turned 80.

In retrospect, I realize turning 80 didn't change me at all. It certainly meant something to other people's perception of me, however. People expect individuals to behave a certain way based off of certain milestones within their life. I don't believe in such limitations. Push past preconceived expectations and don't follow the beaten path.

Practice makes perfect

As a communicator, I have written 29 different books that ultimately all ask the same question. **"What if we could?"**

Sometimes it's necessary to tease, attract, aggravate, and even piss someone off in order for them to step out of their frame of reference. This revelation takes me back to a story I often like to share.

When I was 12, my father moved our family from New Jersey to California to get into the furniture business in 1948. My Uncle Ralph had given me a saxophone and I had been taking lessons in New York. Before our departure to California, my Saxophone teacher told me to look up Moore Johnson, his previous teacher and mentor. He explained Moore was one of the best Saxophone players in the entire world. Moore didn't teach kids but my teacher was confident he would make an exception for me.

Once we settled into our new home, my parents and I made the trip out to Hollywood so we could meet Moore Johnson. We pulled up to his studio one morning. It was dark and cluttered. A single light bulb suspended by a chain from the ceiling.

I still remember surveying Moore for the first time. He was quite short and very fat. His bloated neck was stuffed into a maroon button up silk shirt that held up his round, red face. His ears were pasted back against his head and he observed my family with beady little eyes.

"You must be Mr. and Mrs. Gerber," he introduced himself to my parents. "And you must be Michael," he said before ushering me into the darkness from whence he came. Then, Moore instructed me to play from a book placed on a music stand. After only a minute he stopped me.

Moore walked me back out to my parents and told them he would teach me with a few stipulations. I was to practice three hours a day, five days a week, without question. Moore then handed my parents a copy of the bus schedule, explaining I was to take the bus to our scheduled meetings. Last, Moore explained he didn't want to see my parents again. He said I was bound to complain about his teachings at some point but that was between him and me.

Well, my parents weren't exactly certain of these arrangements "Are you sure you want to do this?" My father asked with concern.

"Yes," I responded immediately.

After that, we said our farewells to Moore and drove home. Practicing fifteen hours a week may seem like a daunting task for a 12-year-old but I was confident in myself. I was a natural on the Saxophone. I knew if it took someone three hours to practice, I could easily put in fifteen minutes a day and yield the same results. The best part of all, was that my parents would never know if I was practicing the amount I pledged to Moore. They had their own life to live and would be none the wiser.

I practiced a grand total of roughly three hours that entire first week before I met with Moore again. I sat down in Moore's chair and we began our lesson. I played for only a few seconds before Moore told me to put my horn down.

"What did I tell you last week?" he asked. "I only want to teach people who strive to be the best saxophone players in the world. I told you how long you should practice and you didn't do that. Get your ass home and make up your mind if this is something you want to pursue. If you're really serious about learning the saxophone, I will see you the same time next Saturday."

I was absolutely floored on the bus ride home. No one had ever spoken to me like that before. Not my parents, not my teachers, not even my old saxophone teacher in New York.

I now realize the context of the exercise wasn't to illustrate if I liked to practice or not. Moore was trying to determine if I had the discipline to work towards being one of the best saxophone players in the world. He wanted me to showcase if I was capable of following a set of rules within the process.

Moore taught me a valuable lesson that shaped me into the man I am today. You have to be willing to push beyond what's ordinary to achieve something extraordinary. Without context, the practice was just practice. It was empty of meaning until I understood why I was putting in the necessary time.

> You have to be willing to push beyond what's ordinary to achieve something extraordinary.

How to discover meaning within your own life

The best advice I can give anyone is to become a great student. Learn something you can practically utilize. The greatest experience in my life was studying the saxophone. It wasn't the outcome of becoming a really good saxophone player that gave me meaning in my pursuit. It was honing my craft during the journey and practicing three hours a day.

Find something to practice in your pursuit of the impossible. Discover the process of learning through exercise and repetition. Young people need to stick to commitments and practice to become extraordinary.

The #1 best thing you can do right now to get ahead

There's a completely underutilized treasure trove of information that people use less and less. It's called *READING*!

You'd be absolutely flabbergasted by how many people who have read one of my books approach me to tell me it's the first book they have ever read in their whole life. It's completely astonishing.

"How did you make it through school," I always think. These individuals must have faked their way through the system. The problem is they are denying themselves the opportunity to grow.

Ever since a young age, I always read, as it took me to another world in my pursuit of finding answers and meaning in life. I highly encourage you to read as well. It's a valuable resource that doesn't require capital. Educating yourself will help develop your potential, giving you an edge in life.

It's easy to do. I'd suggest finding an author whose work captures your attention. Dedicate yourself to reading all of the material they've written. If that one book connected with you just imagine the potential goldmine of information the rest of their work can contain. I've published multiple books myself and haven't met someone who has read all of them, despite the many praises people may sing of my work.

It's also critical to practice the information digested from reading, regardless of what it is. Excel with practice. I'd recommend finding other people you can talk to about what you've learned through your readings. It's important to engage in what you're learning. Immerse yourself in new ideas, language, and meaning. Dive deeper past superficial meanings to absorb the deeper contents.

The meaning of life

Everyone strives to find meaning in life. My journey has always been in the pursuit of meaning. I found that meaning in creation.

I like to think that we are all made in God's image. By the transitive property, that must mean mankind was born to create. I want to believe every human being is born with the same ability to mold ideas into existence. To create is divine. It's important to realize discipline is critical to truly experience life. Discipline requires adhering to the rules. Unfortunately, most people won't discover the rules developed from rigorous practice. Instead, they sit idly with their self-developed rule set. Others refuse to adopt a more successful structured system and thus change into a more complete person.

My advice is to follow instructions and appreciate the process.

Practice makes perfect.

In the pursuit of perfection, the meaning of life will be revealed.

> It's important to realize discipline is critical to truly experience life. Discipline requires adhering to the rules.

Chapter 2

You Need to Get Your Hands Dirty

An Interview with Mitch Free, Entrepreneur & Digital Manufacturing Expert

How Mitch became an entrepreneur

I am a bit of an unlikely entrepreneur. I always thought I wanted to be an engineer, but I only lasted in college four weeks. I didn't know how to study. School had always come easily to me, to the point I didn't have to study, but college moved at a different pace. I dropped out and thought, "I'm going to refocus and return with a vengeance. I'm going to study, but in the meantime, I'm going to get a job and start working."

At 18, I started manufacturing work and found it fascinating. I decided a better scholastic route for me would be to pursue trade school, so I signed up and completed a one-year course in manufacturing technology. Upon graduation, I began working for a company that made automotive stamping dies and machined aerospace components. Of course, the trade school certificate only gave me the right to start at the bottom. Within six months, I regretted my decision. This job required a lot of tedious manual labor, not the sexy stuff. It would take years to get to that level.

However, just as a I was about to give up and go back to college, the company received a contract that required the purchase and implementation of programmable automated machinery, and much of the older staff was intimidated and didn't want to learn a new technology. One day, the company owner approached me with a question: "Do you have an interest in learning computers and robotics?"

> "Do you have an interest in learning computers and robotics?"

"Absolutely," I said.

I quickly discovered I had a real aptitude for the work. After five years at the leading edge of manufacturing technology, I was recruited to set up manufacturing operations within a major airline and quickly rose up the ladder.

Next, I spotted an opportunity to enter the 3D CAD software business in the late 90's as it was transitioning to PC's. This parlayed me into founding a global internet business, MFG.com, a world-wide marketplace for manufacturing that facilitates billions of dollars in manufacturing transactions.

The eureka moment

When it came to my 3D CAD software, I had customers on both sides of the equation. Engineers used the technology to design products. Meanwhile, manufacturers used it to aid them in the manufacturing process. When I brought my customers together for events to learn my software, I noticed they seemed to care more about networking and collaborating on projects. My design customers would often ask me, "We've got this new product coming out. Do you know who can manufacture it for us?" Vice versa, my manufacturing customers would ask, "We've got open manufacturing capacity, do you know anyone that needs manufacturing?"

In 1999, I scheduled a lunch to connect some of my design clients with a couple of my manufacturing clients. While driving out of the parking lot, I happened to hear a radio commercial for lendingtree.com (an online loan marketplace) that said "request your mortgage and let lenders compete."

It was my eureka moment. I thought, Holy smoke. What if factories and shops competed for orders?

So, over a long weekend, I wrote the first version of MFG.com. Initially I assumed it would be a community builder for my 3D CAD software business. However, people outside of my software customer base started calling and asking, "Hey, can I join your marketplace?" I said, "Sure, but if you are not my software customer, the cost is $1,000 per year."

Then suddenly they started sending checks! Bam! Calls came in from all over the world. Before I knew it, I had a global marketplace facilitating manufacturing trade worth billions of dollars. It wasn't something I planned, it was an opportunity that arose. I bootstrapped the business, then sold part of it to Jeff Bezos, Amazon's CEO, five-and-a-half-years later.

Brokering a partnership with the CEO of Amazon

In 2005, I had agreed to sell MFG.com to a large public company in France. I had been through months and months of negotiations and due diligence, and we had even agreed on a closing date. Two weeks before closing, I got a call from a man who said, "Hey, I work for Jeff Bezos, and he would like to meet you. Are you going to be in Seattle any time soon?"

I said, "As a matter of fact, I am."

Of course, those weren't my plans at all. However, when Jeff Bezos' people call, you've got to be there. Honestly, at first I thought it might be a prank, but I showed up to the Amazon lobby anyway and told the receptionist I was there to see the man himself.

When she asked if I had an appointment all I could say was, "I think I do." A few minutes later, someone came and took me into a conference room.

> When Jeff Bezos' people call, you've got to be there.

Jeff came in and said, "It's a pleasure to meet you. I'm a big fan of your business." Then he peppered me with questions, non-stop. He wanted to know how I created the company, how I chose the revenue model, and how I envisioned its future.

An hour later, someone came in and said, "Jeff, it's time to go to your next meeting."

Sometime later, I was back at my hotel, wondering what the hell just happened when a lady called me and said, "Jeff would like to be your partner and buy part of the business from you. Did you talk terms?"

I said "No, it wasn't discussed at all". She then said, "I'll take the lead and send you an offer."

I told her that I was flattered but I had already committed to selling the business to someone else. She said she would let Jeff know.

As you can imagine, that only spurred Jeff to send an offer anyway. While the numbers and opportunity to work directly with Jeff Bezos were great, the problem was I had already agreed to sell the company under a binding contract with two weeks to close, so I declined the offer.

Undaunted, Jeff called me a short time later. "Why don't you want to be in business with me?" he asked. He went on to tell me that there were ways to get out of the agreement I had in place to sell my business. He said that he could help me work on that. When I still declined, he said, "Whatever they're paying for your company, I'll pay you $5 million more and hire you to run it for me if that is what you really want. But I think what you want is to take some money off the table to secure your financial future and free your mind to think big and build a world changing business." He was right.

> Think big and build a world changing business.

He was very convincing and generous so I agreed to back out of the deal with the other company prior to closing, chalking it up to seller's remorse. Afterward, I accepted Jeff's offer. I ended up running the company for 13 years, turning MFG.com into a global brand with offices around the world.

Stay nimble, stay little, stay profitable (at least in the beginning)

When building MFG.com, the growing business consumed all the cash it generated. I lived off a meager salary, credit cards and cashed in my 401k to make ends meet. In the early 2000's, when you started an internet business you had to build your own infrastructure. There were no cloud-based hosting services, so you had to buy much of your own hardware, such as servers, firewalls and backup devices. Furthermore, you had to have a team of people ready to manage the hardware.

The barrier to entry was high because of the significant costs necessary to start an internet business, and I wasn't always savvy about raising capital from investors. I had to get creative in order to get around my challenges, which led me to develop a bootstrapping mentality. We would close a sale and buy a stapler, we'd close another and buy a chair. Building the company from profits proved to be a very good approach that forced a lot of discipline and strategic thought.

When you don't have a lot of extra cash, you must make strategic decisions about what will produce value for your customers and how that in turn will return a profit to you. A new company may raise a lot of money at once, hire a bunch of people and get fancy offices, but the costly infrastructure will end up dragging them down before they have a chance to get off the ground.

I prefer the little-engine-that-could approach: put a little coal in the tank as you go. This way, you're financially close with your company, as well as the market. Overfunding a business is counter-productive. When you grow a large team too quickly, the CEO becomes isolated from customers and messages he receives are filtered. The things that initially made the business successful get lost. You must make sacrifices and stay close to the ground in order build a solid foundation and to preserve founder equity. It will exponentially pay off later.

Advice for any entrepreneur starting a new business

You need do something you are passionate about and where you have deep expertise. Most importantly, you have to get your hands dirty in the business. I've never started a business where I didn't initially do everything myself. It is okay to start with a minimally viable product or service. Once you are in the market, listening intently to customers as well as those who don't buy from you will guide your product offering, pricing, and business model in ways you could not have imagined. Don't try and create everything before going to market.

When all that learning paid off

When I sold part of my company to Jeff Bezos, I had very little in my bank account. I remember the day the funds came in. I was sitting in my office, logged into my Bank of America account, refreshing the screen every 90 seconds. Suddenly, the amount went from $500 to several million. Tears started running down my face. This moment was the validation for all my hard work. I had created financial security for myself and for my family. That was a great feeling.

No matter your level of success, there will always be fresh challenges

I have experienced my fair share of struggles and setbacks. For example, getting divorced was painful. To make matters worse, I simultaneously found out I had cancer. At the time I thought, "Oh great, I've worked hard, made good decisions, finally got some money in the bank and then this happens. This was not part of my plan."

Fortunately, the doctors caught my cancer early and I was able to regain my health. I also met the absolute love of my life and remarried. We had a baby, a wonderful daughter who is such an incredible joy. Life is fantastic now, but I will never forget how I felt going through those challenging times. It makes you more appreciative of the little things.

Cultivating the right mindset for risk

Entrepreneurship takes persistence and confidence in your abilities. It also requires a certain mindset regarding failure. I had to get my head around the idea that the worst that can happen is not that bad.

Often, the worst that can happen is bankruptcy. If this happens, it means you will walk away (having learned a ton) and have to seek employment. To be an entrepreneur, you have to be able to bury your head in the sand a little, to not think about all the potential negatives.

> I would rather sit at the bar as an old man, having gotten my ass kicked, than never have played the game.

Instead of worrying about all that can go wrong, you need to be optimistic. Coupled with such positivity needs to be a healthy dose of reality. If you are a Pollyanna, you won't do well.

Be ready to take calculated risks and believe in yourself. For me, the greatest risk is not trying something. I would rather sit at the bar as an old man, having gotten my ass kicked, than never have played the game. I want to have the fewest regrets possible at the end of my life.

What Mitch would tell his 19-year-old self

Start at the ground level, work hard, and treat people well. Any business you work in, have an ownership mentality. Make decisions as if you were the owner and learn all you can about how the business works. Following these steps will prepare you for success. More importantly, the right opportunities will present themselves. Every employer wants employees who think like an owner. These people rise to the top quickly.

Every company needs to innovate, constantly

Things are always changing, whether it be technology, or business models. There are very few businesses that can remain static and stand the test of time. You always have to be innovating and thinking about the future. What will your business look like five years from now? What will your industry be like down the road?

> *Every employer wants employees who think like an owner. These people rise to the top quickly.*

Such uncertainties are often impossible to predict because you don't know what technology, competitors, or alternatives will emerge. Therefore, it is imperative to stay knowledgeable of trends in your industry and adjacent industries. Innovating your business model can be just as important as deploying technology. People are becoming more and more creative with their business models, especially in terms of how they charge or monetize their business. I think some of the greatest innovations coming in the next five years will be in terms of business models.

Also, you always have to earn your profit pool. Whenever incumbent companies enjoy a profit pool for too long without a competitor chasing or pressuring them, they can become lazy and stop finding new ways to create value. This is the number one way to become disrupted. Think about Netflix taking over the market and profits Blockbuster enjoyed for many years. It's important to make sure you're earning your profit pool, otherwise someone is going to take it from you.

To stay current, I suggest experimenting with different technology, apps, and regularly experiencing your own business and similar businesses. You want your customer to be able to better understand what you are providing.

Failure can lead to motivation

We all need significant motivation to drive us. For me, I need to have quite a bit on the line to remain properly motivated. I invest a lot of my own capital and resources into my businesses. And when I add employees, I feel a tremendous obligation to take care of them and their families. I feel equally responsible to investors and customers who invested their hard-earned money in my company, product, or service. I can't let them down. I am driven by my sense of obligation to others. When people believe in me enough to invest in me, come to work for me, or buy from me, I work hard to validate their decision.

Why I once gave away $2 million

Like many startups, MFG.com issued stock options to incentivize employees and reward them for all the hard work and dedication it takes to build a business. When I was in the process of selling MFG.com (before Bezos came along), I had 38 employees. Excited, many of them were already looking at new cars and houses. However, since I didn't end up selling the company like I had originally planned, the stock options were not going to become liquid as they were expecting.

I knew as soon I told my employees about this, I ran the risk of a mutiny. They would be highly disappointed, and I needed to keep the motivation high.

In the process of negotiating my deal with Jeff Bezos, I expressed my concerns which were keeping me up at night. I validated the importance of taking care of them for taking care of me, and believing in me. I told him, "I can't take away the money they are counting on."

We had to find a way to take care of my loyal employees. I never would have thought Jeff would care about something so sentimental, but he said, "That's exactly why I want to be in business with you."

Ultimately, as part of our deal he chipped in $2 million as bonuses for my team. When it came to deciding how to divvy it up, I calculated all of the months everyone had been with me and divided it by the $2 million. (The longer an individual had been with the company the more they were entitled to, regardless of title or function.)

I hosted a company party which many thought was a closing party for the sale of the company. At the party, I informed the group I decided not to sell the company. As to be expected, they immediately panicked.

But then I said, "I didn't forget about you..."

I then played them a video Jeff Bezos had recorded in which he said he was happy to be a partner in our business. People were shocked.

I told them, "Jeff chipped in $2 million. I'm going to distribute now."

After I told them the formula for divvying out the proceeds, one accountant that had been with me since the beginning nearly passed out when she realized her bonus amount. That night changed people's lives. It was the greatest thing to me. I was able to reward great people for their hard work.

The party became known as "The Money Party" and often talked about in the company to inspire new employees and reinforce the culture of taking care of our people.

Mitch's thoughts on the meaning of life

I'm not sure I know. I would like to live a good life, to do well by my family and friends, to try and leave the world a better place than I found it. I also want to raise two well-grounded daughters as productive citizens who make the most out of their lives.

After "The Money Party" when my CFO received her bonus, she gave me a book called Hitchhiker's Guide to the Galaxy that ended with, "The ultimate answer to the ultimate question is the number 42. But what is the question?" The number 42 has always been a recurring theme in my life.

- At the time of the money party, I was 42-years old.
- Jeff Bezos was the 42nd-richest person in the world.

I think the answer to the meaning of life is similar. We don't actually know the ultimate answer to the ultimate question, but we are always in pursuit of it.

> We don't actually know the ultimate answer to the ultimate question, but we are always in pursuit of it.

What adults can learn from today's youth

Today's youth possess a number of attributes that differ from previous generations. One of them is multitasking. They've got their iPads, smartphones, tablets, TVs, radios, and social media channels all going at once. They're able to handle communication and input from multiple sources simultaneously. I am not sure if this skill set can be transmitted to an older generation who didn't grow up with so much stimulus. However, what I do know is harnessing multitasking abilities in creative environments is a powerful advantage.

I also think we can learn about tolerance from today's youth. They are growing up in a more tolerant culture and therefore more accepting of differences regarding race, religion, sexual orientation, etc. I also find they are more self-educated and knowledgeable, even in areas like nutrition. They know how to leverage online content as a tool for learning, bypassing traditional learning methods.

What Mitch wants to be known for

I want to be known as someone who did well, inspired others, and worked hard in an ethical, honest way. I don't care if I become the richest man in the world, I just want to be known for good work and curiosity.

Mitch's biggest role model

There are so many, but I would have to say my father. He was an entrepreneur too, as well as a great inspiration and a good man. The greatest thing he ever did for me was make me believe I could do and be anything I wanted—as long as I was willing to put in the work and make wise life decisions.

Mitch's message to his daughters

I want them to know how much I care about them. I unconditionally love them and will continue supporting them in whatever they wish to do. Whenever life gets them down, I would like to say, "Just wait a minute."

Life constantly changes. We have all been through various cycles, whether they've been business challenges, relationship issues, or health problems. But a month or even a year later, your position in the world is very different.

You can be anything you want – as long as you are willing to put in the work and make wise life decisions.

View life as a marathon, not a sprint. Remember to feed your mind with positivity during those challenging times. And you too can be anything you want—as long as you are willing to put in the work and make wise life decisions.

Chapter 3

What Does Above and Beyond Look Like

An Interview with Dean Del Sesto, Branding Expert & Chief Creative of Venthio, Principal at VeracityColab, Author, Keynote Speaker.

Dean's entrepreneurial instincts appeared early

I started selling candy out of my jacket pocket when I was 12 years old by way of my mother taking me to Pic and Save, now called Big Lots. I bought as much bulk candy as I could, broke apart the packaging, then sold it to kids at school at a net of $20-$30 a week.

I moved to Anaheim Hills, California at age 14. I started selling avocados on the street corner. One day, another kid took my corner, causing sales to tank, so I wrapped up six of my best avocados, went to a local restaurant, and soon landed my first commercial account.

The restaurant kept buying from me season after season, and I started making about $200 dollars per month for the season. In 1980, I started selling my car drawings. Eventually, I screen printed them on coffee cups and sold them to a gift boutique store at a local mall.

Later that year, I contacted a guy my brother partnered with in the auto body business, and we became partners of a small promotional company. We worked together for about 10-12 years and built a decent-sized business with 25 employees. I transitioned from drawing cars to drawing logos and from writing bumper stickers to writing ads. Now fully in the advertising business, I bought him out in 1992 and started another company in 1995 with another partner. That agency became one of the largest advertising companies in Southern California, which ran for 22 years.

Branding companies is my core business. I have branded hundreds of companies in my career, and today I run an agency where we brand about 15-20 companies annually with sales ranging from $10 million to several billion a year. I do everything from market research, positioning, identity, website, collateral design, as well as provide any other company branding needs.

I also am a partner at a video agency called VeracityColab. I joined the team seven years ago, that came from a meeting with three other partners who were making about $250k in sales. I was responsible for the sales strategy, business development, advisory, and I infused some capital into the company. Today, we are one of the largest video agencies in the country. Some of our clients include AT&T, Google, Adobe, Intuit, Thermo Fisher and many other fortune brands. We were recently voted the number one video agency in the country with revenues around $3.5 million.

Overcoming a (normally) devastating financial loss

While I was running my first large agency, we lost two of our biggest clients in a span of three weeks. Within sixty days, our yearly revenue dropped from $15 to $3 million. At the exact time this happened, we were at an interim facility while we were building out a 22 square foot facility we had just bought while shoveling a million dollars into tenant improvements. We had to lay off 50 people in the middle of the process and as a business owner, that hits you hard.

But I've learned to embrace adversity. I believe there is value in it, but will miss the value if I let it eat me up. When I lost those two big clients, I immediately saw it as an opportunity for an adventure. I knew it had happened to either tune me into something or move me from where I was. I didn't want to view it as if my life was over, nor did I want to waste the trial. I saw it as a life-changing, life-giving event; not crashing to an end, but crashing to a new beginning. Change, no matter the magnitude, is never what it is. It's how you relate to it that matters.

Without that loss, I wouldn't have been able to see other opportunities. Since we invested in improving the building, it was worth double what we had paid for it within a year. Plus, I suggested to my business partner that we promote the current employee to the role of president so we could do other things. He eventually bought me out, so I was able to bridge the financial gap and move on to writing, speaking, and doing what I love: branding and helping in the video business.

I also had a pillar of support at home: my wife. Each day I opened up to her about the business. I thought if I did so, she would know how to do two important things: encourage me and pray for me. We've had a great marriage for 24 years, and these discussions brought our relationship to a whole new level. She possesses a tremendous amount of insight because she knows me better than anybody else on the planet. I could always bring her encouragement back to my business, and

> Change, no matter the magnitude, is never what it is.
>
> It's how you relate to it that matters.

this made a normally catastrophic situation an enjoyable business transition.

How Dean balances life, family, and work
When I got married at 30, I reviewed all the areas in my life: my participation in the corporate world, my passions, my family, my wife, my faith, and my physicality. I decided that no one area should suffer at the expense of another. Everything grew a bit slower that way, but every area grew at a healthy pace, so nothing was left behind. I would never leave my wife behind, or let my physicality go, or leave my family, or what I love to do just so one area could thrive.

No one area should mask or stifle the other. I like to have a balance in my marriage and life because then I will always have time, and peace of mind. I also developed a passion to be an advisor and counselor and never say no when anybody asks for help if I'm available. When your life is balanced, you'll have the time to do so and as such, I've logged thousands of hours as a counselor, serve on multiple boards, and get called on frequently for my insights. It's a great deal of fun and fuels the purpose component of me well.

How to mesh creativity with the mechanics of business

if you're a creative person who wants to go into business, you need to build your brand and your position; that space you want to own in the mind of your market. You can't just be 'a creative person' if you want to serve your client(s) in an extraordinary way. You must develop your skill set.

For example, I can go from doing one logo for a company to developing its brand strategy, market research, and marketing planning. That shifts the budget from $25,000 to $1,000,000. I beat out other agencies by not just showing the creative work, but talking strategy and business development. So when I tell clients I can grow their business by 30 percent this year, it becomes a whole other conversation. As for the brand work I do, that's a show and sell business. You show something and it either sells or it doesn't, so the way creatives present their work, online and off, is critical to success.

If you're building a company, you need to carefully select your employees (careful, like doing surgery). You have to dig deep, do a reference check, and create what we call a laboratory experience. We turn interviews into two or three hour-long experiences where we bring an intensity not normally experienced in interviews. In these sessions, we're able to break down any issues and show them the truth of our work culture.

> If you're building a company, you need to carefully select your employees (careful, like doing surgery).

Some of our interviewees have called our process the "best, most challenging experience" they've ever had. We always want to make the right hiring decision not only for our company but for the employees they'll be working with. I've always believed there are no bad employees, just bad hires. By following this unique approach, we also test candidate's defense against mediocrity. We can see how they handle the pressure of day-to-day business in a fast-growing agency. We want someone who has a vision to live out, and we want to give them a try. Again, 100 percent of the candidates that come into this experience, intimidating as it may be, leave our office saying they appreciated it. Sometimes you have to dismantle before you reassemble.

Advice for entrepreneurs about to embark on their first business

Always conduct market research to make sure there's an unmet need or desire in the marketplace for what you produce. Prospects have come to me without their niche or position and I choose to not work with them because I knew I wouldn't be able to serve them well. Instead, I told them to do their research. Many came back a few months later after getting a dose of reality and thanked me because they knew they wouldn't have lasted either.

My next piece of advice would be to be passionate about what you are doing or trash it and do something you love. I loved art and words, so I was able to get into a business which delivered my passion to people. Every time I work with a new client, I'm thrilled by the opportunity to craft words and expressions for the company. If you find this passion, you will find relevance in the marketplace, fulfillment and the money generally follows.

Dean's personal philosophy

I must admit, I was selfish the first 29 years of my life. People were a means to an end. When I met my wife, this mindset changed. I suddenly wanted to give instead of taking. So when I started a new business, I realized I didn't want to live the rest of my life selfishly. I wanted to go into business to serve people, not just my clients, but also my employees and vendors. I valued people over profits because I realized I would

> Money is not the most important part of a business, relationships are. People are more rewarding than money.

Dean Del Sesto

37

profit from those people if I treated them with dignity, respect, and care. Money is not the most important part of a business, relationships are. People are more rewarding than money.

To revolutionize your business, start by serving all people connected to the business the way you would want to be served: be authentic, be genuine, and always be delivering value to other people. Ask yourself these questions when you wake up: what does it look like to serve others today? What does it look like to serve my clients, vendors, alliances, etc.? Deciding these things in advance will determine what kind of day you'll have. Average is over. There is no value in average so status quo is dead. You have to ask: what does above and beyond look like? There is value in serving people extraordinarily in the business world.

Envisioning the future for the next generation of business owners

As strange as it may seem, my vision for the future is right here, right now. My future vision is to maximize the value of present moments. A vision for the future is great but it can be a poison to the present. It can make the present feel empty and if we are focusing too much on the future we will blast past all that is rich, relevant, and candidly in need of our presence.

Visualizing in today's day age is also different. We live in a different world than we did 20 or 30 years ago. There is a lot of political and economic volatility. The media has exposed us to most of it; one acronym I give for media is that it Moves Everyone Directly Into Anxiety. Media stresses us out so the way that we intake it is extremely important to our peace of mind. Of course, there have been and will continue to be difficult economic times, like the bust in 2008—a difficult time for us as well—but I think the future looks very bright for young people.

> It suddenly became real where recognition was given for performance, not just participation. It's much more competitive than they ever realized.

I recently heard someone speak at my church about the challenges millennials face. He mentioned a dangerous drug known as "affirmation." By now, everyone knows how millennials received trophies and participation ribbons no matter how well they performed. Parents thought they could mask the pain of losing by keeping their children as comfortable as possible.

Unfortunately, when these millennials grew up, life hit them with a violence they weren't quite expecting. So, for many millennials, life is not necessarily what they thought it was going to be. It suddenly became real where recognition was given for performance, not just participation. It's much more competitive than they ever realized. They also learned that unless they did an incredible job, they weren't likely to get noticed.

Dean Del Sesto   39

I think this upcoming generation will have to rise higher than before. Knowing this, it's important to realize that hard work, discipline, and serving others is the best way to stay relevant and viable in our dynamic workplace. If you don't implement these skills, if you don't push yourself, you will more likely be left behind.

To me, hard work is identifying what would be of exemplary value to someone you are serving, then delivering it. Model this, and always go a little beyond what is expected. If you remember this in every situation, then you will earn more clients, more followers, and more of everything. In contrast, those that do enough to make ends meet will generally meet the end soon.

As for standing out as a personal or business brand we are over-saturated with information. Every day, approximately 500 new websites launch into the "datmosphere." Hundreds of blogs try to gain popularity. More and more distribution channels pop up for news, media, and content. We're suffering from this thing called 'communication fatigue' or 'content stress syndrome.'

We exist in a world with a lot of noise. It's not as easy to stand out as it was 50 years ago. Today, everything is good. You have to "kill it" in every aspect of what you do just to compete.

> It's not as easy to stand out as it was 50 years ago...you have to "kill it" in every aspect of what you do just to compete.

Characteristics entrepreneurs need to be successful

You have to care like crazy. If you don't, you need to find a non-entrepreneurial, going through the motions job. Caring is foundational to being in business. In fact, you have to care so much that it's almost alarming. Caring shows up in all areas of what we do. For example, technology is changing so quickly that you have to care enough each day to stay ahead of what's current. Otherwise, you will become obsolete within a year and you'll have to admit it to yourself that you just didn't care enough to stay current.

Next, you need to surround yourself with amazing people in your life—this is paramount. There's another saying for this: "Your growth is contingent upon the books you read and the people you meet."

About 20 years ago, I joined a Christian CEO forum called Convene. I stayed in it for 12 years, and it ended up being part of the top three catalytic events of my life. It transformed me into a more effective human being because I learned from a diverse group of people.

Although I am not in Convene anymore, I serve on the Board of Directors, I am an approved Convene speaker and I am an anchor in one of their CEO groups. As such, I'm still learning through close proximity to learn from really smart people. I get to use my own gift to speak into their lives. It's a win/win everywhere.

Part of equipping yourself for business is surrounding yourself with like-minded people. I think everyone should have a mentor in their lives, or at least others who are willing to give them advice when needed. I have dozens, and I leverage those relationships often.

Dean Del Sesto

> I think everyone should have a mentor in their lives, or at least others who are willing to give them advice when needed. I have dozens, and I leverage those relationships often.

Many people don't realize how willing others are to talk about themselves and their work (which, in turn, will help you). As long as you're humble, don't be afraid to call somebody more successful who you think may not have the time. When I was running my agency, I used to call big agency owners and tell them, "I've got a small agency that makes about $6 million a year. I really respect your business and like the work you guys are doing. Can I take you out for coffee to get some advice on some things?" Nobody ever said no to me, and if they did, I probably wouldn't want to meet with them anyways.

The ability to gracefully seek out people you respect is one of the best qualities you can possess. I always tell the young adults I counsel: make it a point to meet with 2-3 people per month. At the end of the year, you will have met 24-36 people who have either given you counsel or created more opportunities. People are the conduit. You have to get used to professionally interacting with them. Yeah, every conversation has equity within. Every formed relationship can be invested in any number of future situations.

Knowing how to communicate and navigate relationships is the most powerful entrepreneur tool, so you should make a point to learn and understand personality styles.

There are four different ones: choleric, phlegmatic, melancholy, and sanguine.

Cholerics like to take control and need bottom-line communication. Melancholies are analytic; they want to know the details of the details. The more they know, the better. Sanguines relate to the party-types; they are happy, outgoing, and like to keep the final prize in mind. Phlegmatics are supportive. They want to know all of the mechanics and what it will take exactly to make it work. This is a cursory evaluation of course.

But when I understood these different styles of people, I could go into a room, and knowing who was going to be responsible for what, I could present to a large executive board. I would address each individual personally, hitting on what would be important to them based on their personality type and or role. My closing percentages based on those individualistic pitches dramatically rose, and my ability to use my creativity pushed through deals better, faster, and easier. I didn't get into as many conflicts, because I addressed these people in the way that worked for them, spoke in their language, and made them feel valued. There is no scientific formula for communication, but you need to speak in a way that is uniquely relevant to your listeners. Adaptation is key. Your personal style alone is not enough.

Speak in a way that is uniquely relevant to your listeners. Adaptation is key. Your personal style alone is not enough.

What Dean wants to be known for

Being a great husband, a man who lived out his Christianity to an honest, tangible extent, and one who cared deeply to make a difference in the lives of other people by helping them live a life to their full potential.

I am grateful I integrated counseling and advisory work into the confines of my corporate schedule because I wouldn't be able to have the relationships I have today; nothing would be the same. I wouldn't have had the kind of fulfillment I had without those relationships.

I have also found it rewarding to keep my word and commitments, even though it's a high bar and requires sacrifice at times to do so. We all break commitments from time to time. Instead of blowing it off and not keeping your word, renegotiate your commitment with others prior to the deadline, and you'll always be able to keep your integrity.

The sustainability of the value you experience in your life is going to be largely contingent upon the level of character and integrity you exercise. Nobody owns integrity, you can't possess it, but you can practice it.

> Integrity is an ongoing process that describes the totality of your character system in play, not just the convenient areas.

You can't claim, "Hey, I have integrity," because, in some way, you'll be out of integrity before the day is over.

Integrity is an ongoing process that describes the totality of your character system in play, not just the convenient areas. That's known as selective virtue or circumstantial integrity which is meaningless to everybody. I'm not perfect, but I love practicing a high level of ongoing integrity in my life. I sleep better at night.

Altruism is what makes life meaningful

About 15 years into my marriage, my wife said, "You have a way with younger people." I never thought I'd be a counselor, but one day I prayed about it and made a deal with God that if he brought me people that I would do well with, I would never say no. That was my deal. Three months later, I was working with four different people: one had a drug addiction, another struggled in their marriage, and the other two felt trapped in their business. Since then, I've worked with hundreds of people. Sometimes they call me out of the blue and ask to meet. This is what makes life fulfilling for me.

I can utilize my training in business, as an author and a speaker. I am then able to help people, even in situations I haven't been professionally versed in. I've been blown away by the successes, but not surprised because it's my calling and I am privileged to do so.

Even though most people start doing things of significance where they use their gifts, talents, and abilities later on in life, I believe every young person should integrate their unique gifting. This way, they can develop their skills and get some experience. So, by the time they reach that real wisdom age, they can hit the ground impacting lives at an even greater level as they develop more free time.

> At the end of the day, life is about giving.

At the end of the day, life is about giving. It's about creating so much value for people that you get to see your value show up in the lives of other people, and that provides great rewards that are lasting.

Chapter 4

If the Worst People Can Do or Say is 'No', You've Got to Go for It

An Interview with Joe Garner, six-time New York Times Best-Selling Author

What it feels like to learn you are a *NY Times Best Selling Author*

You have to understand, I had no expectations. I was in Chicago, Illinois, staying at the Marriott on Michigan Avenue. I'll never forget it. I'd just finished an interview and had gone back to the hotel. I was getting ready to go out again for a book signing. All of a sudden, I get a knock on the door. I look through the peephole, and it's a bell man, carrying a bucket of Champagne.

He came in, and the first thing I said is, "Do you have the right room? I didn't order any Champagne."

Joe Garner

"No, this is the right room," he said.

He set it down and left. Now I'm by myself. I looked at the card. It was from my publisher. It read: 'Congratulations. You're a *New York Times Bestselling Author*.'

> I looked at the card. It was from my publisher. It read: 'Congratulations.
>
> You're a *New York Times Bestselling Author*.'

I didn't know what to do because I just couldn't imagine that. So, I did what I thought I should do. I uncorked the champagne, opened the blinds to see all of the city, and toasted Chicago for sharing the news with me.

What it feels like to learn you are a *NY Times Best Selling Author* for the second, third, fourth and fifth time

The feeling is extreme gratitude, of course. However, the process of reaching that achievement becomes a bit of an an addiction. The drug becomes Amazon. It's a horse race. You put out a new book, and then once it's been released you start doing media for it. Then you return to Amazon after each appearance or interview to see the effect it had - or didn't - on the books ranking.

At a certain level, it starts becoming a barometer of what the sales are around the country. So then you start wondering, 'Are we close? Are we close?'

Finally, when you get that phone call and the person says, "You've made it," it's pretty heady.

When I put my second book out, it was Christmas time. We were at a party, and when I came back there was a voicemail waiting. It was from my publisher.

"Well, I've got good news and I've got better news! Your new book is on the *New York Times Bestseller's List* and the popularity has brought last year's book back on the *New York Times Bestseller's List*. So, you're starting the new year with <u>two</u> books on the *Bestseller List* simultaneously."

You just get giddy at that point. It's like, "What? *How did this happen!?*"

How Joe became a writer

I am sort of an accidental author in the sense that I had zero aspirations growing up to become an author. I always had a passion for pop culture, history, and broadcast journalism-- especially how broadcast media affected history. So, that's where my passions lay.

I was with Dick Clark Productions, and then I went into radio. I was with Westwood One Radio Networks when I came up with my first book idea. It was back in 1998, and everybody was talking about the millennium. As a network, we were trying to figure out how to acknowledge the passing of the 20th century into the 21st century. The company had amassed a sizable archive of radio broadcasts. Naturally, we were going to create these little vignettes of landmark moments, and then use our broadcasts as a way to entertain and inform people.

I got back to my office, and I was just struck by how everybody in that meeting had a story to tell about where they were when big moments in history occurred:

- The Kennedy assassination,
- The Apollo 11 Moon Landing,
- The Gulf War.

It occurred to me that they were more than just defining moments in history. They were the benchmarks of our lives. The where-were-you-when moments.

The other common denominator was that all these events were introduced to us with the same four chilling words: '**We interrupt this broadcast**...'

"Damn," I thought. "This is a great idea for a book!"

It also occurred to me we live in such a wonderful age because our history is literally recorded. I could include the actual broadcast bulletins on audio CDs, tucked into the back cover. My idea was to create a nice big coffee table book filled with stories surrounding these events from a broadcast perspective with the actual real-life photographs, the iconic photographs that people remember that are inextricable from the moment.

It was just one of those turning points where you think, "God, maybe I ought to do something with that idea someday."

On persistence

You can't let other people's opinions drown out your inner passion. I've always lived by the creed that the worst people can say is 'no', so why not? I didn't know the first thing about the publishing business when I became an author the first time. I just picked a book off my desk that was about broadcast history, looked up the publisher, and started making cold-calls.

One cold-call led to the next one, which led to the next one, which led to the next one. After I'd plowed through just about every publishing firm in the New York City, I finally found a little publisher out of Naperville, Illinois, that I was introduced to by a mutual friend.

She looked at me by the end of our meeting and said, "Joe, I'll publish this book on one condition."

"What's that?"

"That you agree to go out and promote it. Because if you're selling me, you'll sell the American people."

Believe in yourself. Believe in your visions.

When I started telling my friends and family that I was going to write a book they said, "Okay, but don't you think you ought to try reading one first?"

The thing is, I had a vision. *I saw this book.* I knew what it looked like. I just decided this was what I was going to do. I spent the next 8 or 9 months doing it, and in the process, I knew I needed someone special for the book. The book's concept, content, and title, were spot on, I thought, but I wanted a name on that cover that really spoke to people in terms of broadcast history.

At the time, Walter Cronkite was still alive and, of course, he's the gold standard. He still is, even today. So, I wrote him a letter. I knew of him, but I didn't know him. And I didn't know anybody else who did.

In my head, I thought: 'The worst he can say is no."

About ten days later I received a phone call from his Chief of Staff saying that Walter Cronkite would be happy to provide the forward to the book! We published the book in October of '98 and by December it hit the *New York Times Bestseller List.* It just changed the whole trajectory of my life and career.

Joe Garner

What to do when people tell you no

When people say 'no' to me, I try and evaluate if they truly gave it any sort of consideration. It really depends on who you hear 'no' from.

Sometimes, there are gatekeepers. Gatekeepers say no because it's easier to say 'no' than to say, "Well, let me look into it," or "Can you give me more information?'"

Let me give you an example. My second book was sports-themed. Naively, I thought it would be pretty much the same routine as creating my book about news moments. So, I sat down with Louise Argianis, the head of Rights and Clearances from ABC Sports.

I said, "Louise, I'm thinking about doing a sports edition of this book."

She shook her head. "I can't believe you're going to try this."

"What's the difference?" I asked.

"The difference is the ownership of the news is ours. It's at our discretion, but when it comes to the play-by-play, the ownership is shared between the leagues and the networks. Before we can even begin to negotiate with you, you're going to have to be licensed and/or sanctioned by Major League Baseball, the NFL, the NBA, the National Hockey League, and the USOC. I also see you have the 1980 Wimbledon Men's Singles Championship final on your list, so the All-England Lawn and Tennis Club is going to have to have approval rights, too."

I said, "Okay, if I can get all those rights, then will you license me the material?"

She agreed, so my next call was to Deanna, her colleague at CBS Sports. The woman wouldn't take my call. I even phoned at different times of the day in hopes I would catch her off-guard.

Finally, I did, but she immediately dismissed me. "Joe," she said. "We would never participate in a project like this. Nor will any of the other networks."

I told Deanna I realized I had perhaps caught her at an inopportune time. "But will you give me 15 more seconds so I can tell you about my conversation with your colleague over at ABC?"

As soon as I did, there was a long pause. Then she said, "We'll do whatever ABC does." The same thing happened over at NBC, and the rest is history.

The good Lord looks after the ignorant and persistent, and if you're the right mix of both, you can be very successful.

I've heard no before, but I always go back and think: 'Why did I get that no? What information didn't I provide? Also, is this something that's really important to me? Is this something that's a true passion, or am I just trying to achieve a shortcut here?'

I've always found that in situations where you've done your homework, and the other person understands your authenticity and true passion, it's very difficult to say no to that. However, if you go in just doing something for the money, then expect the no. They can smell it a mile away.

The need for supportive parents: (I'm not sure I agree with this heading. Not everyone will have "supportive parents". Maybe "The benefit of supportive parents"

I was blessed with supportive parents. I was surrounded by powerful, positive thinking that influenced me. My Dad was a salesman, so it was just natural that would be the kind of pervasive mentality in our household.

As a nine year old, growing up in the corn fields of Illinois, I had aspirations of being in the entertainment business. My parents always encouraged me. They didn't indulge me, but they didn't dissuade me either.

I'm lucky enough to have that memory, where I learned the worst people can do is say is no, so you've got to go for it.

To make a very long story short, the only brush with show business I had growing up in Central Illinois was on an annual trip we would make up to Milwaukee, Wisconsin, for the home office meeting that my Dad's company held every year.

The year was 1969, so if you Google it, you'll discover one of the biggest stars on the planet at the time was a comedian by the name of Bob Hope, and he was hosting this event. In my nine-year-old logic, I knew I had to meet him! Somehow, that meeting was going to inspire and motivate me to new heights.

> The year was 1969, so if you Google it, you'll discover one of the biggest stars on the planet at the time was a comedian by the name of Bob Hope.

So, I sat down and wrote a letter to the president of Northwestern Mutual Life Insurance, my Dad's company. Now, my parents could have been naysayers; they could have said, 'Don't do that' for any number of reasons, or just simply out of embarrassment.

They didn't.

I sent the letter, explaining that my Dad had always encouraged me to go after goals and that meeting Bob Hope was my goal. I don't have the original letter anymore, but the letter I do have is the one I got back from Frances E. Ferguson, the president of Northwestern Mutual Life Insurance about two weeks later.

"I would be happy to help you meet your goal," he wrote. He also gave me the logistics. "Come out to Brewer Stadium for our event. You and your Dad will get to stand on second base where you'll meet Mr. Hope."

Now, Brewer Stadium is a major league baseball stadium. It's absolutely huge. When I gave my Dad the news, his jaw just hit the ground. So, we went there and it was incredible. All these cars began pulling up outside as we entered. *Boom, boom, boom*, went the fanfare. All hell broke loose. There were so many arrangements, so many lights and cameras. And out of it all, appeared Bob Hope in the flesh. *The Bob Hope.*

At the appointed time, they took me into the locker room where I met him. To this day, when I smell cigar smoke, it always puts me back in that place.

"You must be Joe," Bob Hope said, shaking my hand.

From there, how do you *not* think anything's possible?

You can't teach drive

I have to give credit to my parents. My Dad helped me prepare for the very first job interview I ever went to. At the time he said, "Now, Joey, I want you to close your eyes and imagine you're in that room. I want you to imagine you're shaking hands with the interviewer. Imagine what that's like. You're going to give him a firm handshake and you're going to look him in the eyes."

So, I had a great tutor, but my life has also been very trial and error. Just trying things out and seeing that, more often than not, things work out. I've tried to reverse-engineer it, and that's the closest I can come to splitting the atoms and figuring out where drive comes from.

My Dad also used to say something else that is not politically correct these days. "The average person is just that. Average. If you're determined to be more than average, then you must decide you're not going to leave work at 5-o-clock like everybody else."

When I worked at Dick Clark Productions, I left at 5 or 6 p.m. each day, unless they were working on a show. But then I found Dick's tape vault in the office. I went in there, set up the video machine, and pulled out all his demo reels. I watched the shows that were successful to learn the formula. But I especially paid attention to the shows that bombed or never got off the ground. I wanted to learn from those too.

It's largely a matter of taking advantage of opportunities you're given, no matter how small. The smallest advantage can have the greatest impact.

Ultimately, it's about having a good work ethic. It comes down to recognizing the fact that you have a DVR, so you don't have to run home to catch your show. Catch it later so you can seize every opportunity. At the same time, life balance matters. But balance is not as easy to pull off, especially if you really wish to succeed as an entrepreneur.

My Dad used to say, "I wake up 'unemployed' every day." He

> My Dad used to say, "I wake up 'unemployed' every day."

had a great career, but he was in sales. When you're in sales, you're an entrepreneur. You just wake up every morning thinking, "I'm unemployed. I have to do something today to improve the situation, to improve my business, to take it to the next level."

When you get it to the level that you really want to be at, and I don't know what that is, you'll know it. I've seen it in people.

Do what you love. Love what you do. Passionately! My Dad worked hard. He had a depression-era mentality. He was out there every day, but he also did it because he loved it. He was in the insurance business, but he wasn't selling insurance, he was helping you plan your life.

When you approach your existence from that level, it's a whole different ball game. I don't care what you do. If you're building widgets or selling them, it doesn't matter. There's a great Ted Talk with Simon Sinek in which he says, "People don't buy *what* you do, they buy *why* you do it."

> There's a great Ted Talk with Simon Sinek in which he says, "People don't buy *what* you do, they buy *why* you do it."

Strive to make a difference with your life's work

Seek your higher purpose. Admittedly, the reasons for creating my first book were selfish. I just didn't understand at the time that these moments that I was collecting were really a scrapbook of all our lives.

I found that out when I was doing a radio interview one time for the second book. The radio personality said to me out of the blue, "Joe, the greatest day I ever spent with my Dad in this life was with your book."

"Wow, that's pretty incredible," I said. "What do you mean by that?"

"My Dad and I never really had much of a relationship, but the one thing we shared was sports," he said. "It was Christmas day. He was dying. He was in his bedroom, and I bought him a copy of *And The Crowd Goes Wild*. I was sitting next to his bed, and we were just kind of leafing through the book and listening to the broadcast, and it was just such a close moment for us."

I thought, that's it! That's what I've got to do. I'm creating these books to help people collect their memories and to experience these moments together.

Handling unforeseen obstacles

As an entrepreneur, you're going to encounter unexpected obstacles and unexpected experiences. There's no way to be an entrepreneur and have every single thing planned out.

If I'd have known every way I could have failed, if I knew there were 400,000 non-fiction books published every year, I would have said to myself, "Well, that's a pretty good idea, Joe, but I don't know if you should go through with this."

> If I'd have known every way I could have failed, if I knew there were 400,000 non-fiction books published every year ...

And yet, there's almost nothing I love hearing more than, *"Oh, you're not going to get that done! That's not going to happen. They're not going to agree to that!"*

As I mentioned, you're going to encounter experiences you're not anticipating as an entrepreneur. Let me give you an example from my own life involving a movie star, Dustin Hoffman. What I always tried to do with the talent that I worked with on all of my books was to at least have one meet and greet; a little hello or something before we actually began working together.

I wrote a book titled *Now Showing Unforgettable Moments from The Movies*. Just as the title indicates, all the stories are about these moments that have become iconic for one reason or another, and it included the actual clips from the films.

I wanted to get somebody who was inextricable from people's memories of movies as the narrator of the DVD. At the top of my list was Dustin Hoffman. To make a long story short, I wound up getting him to agree, but his schedule didn't permit me to say hello or anything before the day we were supposed to work together.

Now, I had heard many stories about how temperamental Dustin was. You know, all these kinds of things people say. On the day we began shooting at this little studio in Hollywood, all of a sudden, panic hit me. *I'm going to be directing an Academy Award-winning actor. What was I thinking?*

So, we're all set, and I hear Dustin has arrived. I calm myself and walk into the makeup room. He's sitting there and I say, "Dustin? I'm Joe Garner. I'm so glad you agreed to do this. How do you want to work together? Do you want to self-direct? I don't mind."

He put his hand up. "Joe. This is your project. I'll do whatever you tell me to do."

And from that moment on, it was fine. But, whew, boy! *The anticipation.* What I've found is that often times, the anticipation is much worse than the reality of something.

To be sure, I also had the competence to pull off the shoot because I was prepared. I'd gone through every script. I knew where I wanted him to stand. I knew the inflections I needed. So, what transpired in my mind was, "Okay, you're prepared for this!" And ultimately, it was a great experience.

Yes, there are jerks out there

The reality is you're going to encounter difficult personalities. It's not your fault. You can't take it personally. You have to understand that their life path allowed them to experience things that turned them into a curmudgeon. (Or insert your own synonym here.)

That's just the way it is. I've always found that if you prepare ahead of time, you are better able to handle these types of challenging situations. Preparedness is everything. Always do your homework.

On facing adversity and struggle

When I was with the radio network, we had a new CEO come in. Basically, the bottom line of my division was not the bottom line he envisioned. So, I was unceremoniously let go. Meanwhile, I had one child in private school, two cars, a mortgage, and I had a wife who was six months pregnant.

It's really important to have a support system if you can because I got home and immediately began making plans. I was scared to death. But at the same time my wife knew I had this idea for *We Interrupt this Broadcast*. For whatever reason—and I do have to give her credit for this—in her condition she could have easily just said, "You can find another job in broadcasting, this is L.A.," but she didn't.

Instead, she said, "Why don't you pursue your idea?"

My wife knew I was always entrepreneurially inclined. Even when I was with the network, I got tired of the radio business after deregulation. The reality was there was fewer people, and fewer opportunities. Essentially, there was no competition anymore.

Around this same time is when I had my first book idea because the company had amassed such a large archive of material. I went to the company's CEO and said, "I think we can repurpose this content in another fashion outside of the broadcasting business."

Joe Garner   61

I saw the internet as a possibility. I also saw audiobooks as a possibility, and I was able to convince him to believe in my ideas. I was able to switch careers without changing my parking space or even moving my desk.

But what happens when the bottom drops out

Fast forward to 2007. My assistant told me, "You ought to write a memoir."

I naively said, "I think memoirs are only good if there's real adversity and struggle in one's life. I don't feel like I've had that many struggles."

Well, it was as if God heard that and said "Oh yeah! I forgot the adversity."

Bang! Along came the downturn in the economy. *Bang!* Large-covered books aren't going to be sold anymore because people can't afford them. *Bang!* Let's rip up the real estate market in Southern California.

My house plummeted in value. Then my wife left me and our kids. Suddenly, I became the single father of two children. Google became my new best friend. I never cooked. So I had to learn. We would be in the middle of talking, and I would have to excuse myself.

"I have to go into my office to check on something," I would say. Then I would Google how to cook some element of dinner.

Here's the important thing to remember: *this too shall pass.* I thought I had to get outside of myself to deal with my adversity. The way I got out of focusing on myself was to focus on my two kids. I made sure their worlds were stable and ensured their routine continued to my best ability. So that was my salvation. Faith, perseverance, believing in myself, and focusing on them.

Stay optimistic. Even when you're going through hell

Sometimes, those storm clouds don't look like they're going to part anytime soon, but they will. That's what I knew, and that's how I stayed focused on my kids when things reached their lowest point.

Just keep going. Get up tomorrow and keep doing it. It's all in the attitude and how you look at things. If you're expecting negativity, that's what you will draw to you. If you look at the universe and see an evil, destructive, and hard place, that's all you're going to experience. If you don't believe that, then you're being foolish.

What it means to be an entrepreneur

Being an entrepreneur is freedom, but with freedom comes responsibility. You have to be disciplined. There is the possibility of great reward, achievement, and success if you are brave.

I can't tell you how many friends of mine are working in jobs they completely hate. I can't even imagine that.

Sure, you have to work hard, you have to be disciplined. But man! Being an entrepreneur can give you a lot of freedom.

> Being an entrepreneur can give you a lot of freedom.

Elevate your game

I had the good fortune to work with famed sportscaster Bob Costas several times. Larry King used to have a show on CNN, and I was on it with Bob. I remember sitting down in that chair and thinking to myself. "Oh, my God, that's Bob Costas sitting next to me!"

It made me want to sit up a little straighter, and be a little more articulate. I encourage everyone to surround themselves with people you aspire to be like.

Don't just surround yourself with people at your age and stage in life. Try to surround yourself with people that are ahead of you on the career track. Because then you have to elevate your game. It strengthens you.

The struggles and joys of being a writer

While I can't hold a candle to his writing, I subscribe to something Ernest Hemingway used to say, "I hate to write, but I love to have written."

That's where I come from. I have an idea and I know what I want to say. I try to say it to the best of my ability. I know where my strengths and weaknesses are. I'm an idea guy. I can come up with them, and I have a sense for what's commercial. I also know how to package concepts and how to infuse them with enthusiasm and authenticity. But I'm not the best writer.

The joy for me, and I've never really taken it for granted, is the opportunity to immerse myself in a completely different world. Most recently, this was in the NASCAR realm.

I tell myself, "Okay. Let me give this a shot, and see what this is about."

I had a similar experience when I wrote my book about Notre Dame Football and got to live on the campus. When I wrote my book about the comedy world, I immersed myself with amazing comedians, and that's been so much fun. The more preparation I do for my next project, the more excited I get thinking, 'I'm really going to get to do this!'

It feels as if I'm playing hooky sometimes. Of course, it's not, and I hope people will be entertained and learn from what I write. But I just pinch myself because I can't believe I'm really here, that I'm really doing this. It's exhilarating.

The most important advice for young people

Don't be afraid.

Fear is paralyzing. The worst thing you can do is be fearful and talk yourself out of something great.

> *Fear is paralyzing. The worst thing you can do is be fearful and talk yourself out of something great.*

I talk about being prepared and that's important, but if you sit there and try to think of every possible way you can fail, trust me, you'll find one.

If you don't have the stomach to be an entrepreneur, maybe you can work for one, even at a startup. And that's fine. Learn from others because there's somebody out there that's already gone down your path.

On Mentorship

I realize we don't all have the benefit of a mentor or a mentoring system but they're out there. You just have to do a little research and find a book or a person and see how they were able to get beyond their fears and limitations.

Living without regret

Make sure you do what feeds your soul. Do something you're passionate about. I've heard from far too many people that didn't. They say things such as, "I have a book I want to write. I've got a great story. There's this book I've always wanted to publish."

I say to them, "Then why don't you do it?"

"Oh, I don't know. It's really hard."

"Just get on a computer," I recommend. "Start writing now. They even have Dragon, this voice recognition program, that allows you to dictate if you can't write. Just do it."

Joe's biggest accomplishment

As a human being, being a father is the most important thing to me. That's my contribution to humanity. And I don't just mean procreating. It's creating two wonderful people, citizens who contribute to society. I would say those are my two proudest moments and accomplishments.

Professionally, I would have to say it's not the *New York Times* accolades or exposure, it's the fact that I entertained people. I gave them enjoyment, they were able to learn something or were inspired by my books.

How to acquire real knowledge in the Information Age

It's incumbent upon you to get your facts. If you want to be part of an informed citizenry, you better get your news from every source possible because it's harder to distinguish now between truth and 'truthiness'. If you only get your news from one source, if you rely on the explosively compressed sources of the cable news networks, then expect to be manipulated.

If Joe woke up penniless and friendless tomorrow, what would he do?

The first thing I would do is seek some sort of shelter. Your heart just breaks every time you see homeless people out there in the elements. So I would take full advantage of whatever the city had to offer. I would get a shower. What's that old expression? If you look sharp, you'll feel sharp.

Then just to get some sort of money coming in, because of my history with radio or television, I would find any radio or television station and beg them into offering me some sort of menial job. Just something to receive money so I could be back around what I am familiar with. I would also write a book proposal about the experience of getting through all of this. Potentially I'd get a publisher interested and get some real money to start over. I even have a tentative book title: *Friendless and Penniless: The Gift of a Clean Slate.*

So that would be my plan.

Joe's Optimism

I know it may look bleak sometimes. I know it looks hard. Maybe you haven't been given the encouragement you deserved, but it's available. It's there. There's light at the end of the tunnel.

You just have to take that first step. Don't be afraid. I promise you, you'll see a break in the clouds.

Try to see the positive in everything, even if it isn't obvious in the moment. I've always been able to take a punch. Of course, it hurts. But it's the same experience every time; no matter what happens, it wasn't as bad as I thought it would be. They haven't taken away my birthday yet. I can still get up. It's cliché but true, attitude is everything!

Joe Garner

You just have to take that first step.

Don't be afraid.

I promise you, you'll see a break in the clouds.

Chapter 5

The Greatest Place to Be in Life Where There's Nothing to Hide

Ted McGrath, Theater Performer, Life Coach, and Professional Storyteller

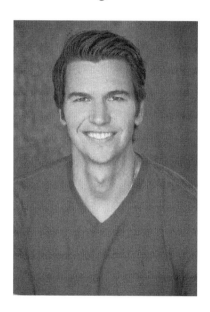

Your life is your message

Everybody has a message. It's your life story. Similar to the mom offering her child advice, or the employee wishing to help a troubled co-worker, many people enter the coaching/speaking world wanting to share their knowledge. They think they have wisdom and expertise to offer. But if you're looking outside of yourself to do so, you're making a big mistake. In order to make the biggest impact with what you share with others, you need to look at your own journey.

Too many people get in my line of work without answering this question: "What's the message other people need to hear?"

The first step needs to involve awareness. The person best suited to give society advice is someone who is aware. There's so much you can learn from observation. My life's work is to look at my story, at my personal journey, and ask, "What did I learn and how might I share it with others so they don't make the same mistakes?"

On giving advice

When people come to me for advice, I turn the question around. I ask them: "What do *you* really want out of your life?" Most people don't know.

"What do *you* really want out of your life?"

This is my response. "Here's what I learned. Avoid this trap. There's something deeper for you. You have a story. You have a message. Transform your life. Become a responsible member of society, *then* serve others and pass on your knowledge and wisdom.

How I decided to become an entrepreneur.

When I was six years old, my Dad walked into the living room one day and said, "Your Mom and I are getting a divorce."

That was a hard thing to accept. As a little kid, I thought, "My parents don't love me." After that, I turned into this little achiever. I decided if I just worked hard enough and became successful, my parents would approve of me and love me.

Beginning at an early age, I started living in this unconscious pattern of 'achieve, achieve, achieve.' I did everything I could to be number one. By the time I was 21, I entered the professional world, working for a company called New York Life Insurance.

My boss was about only about 5'8" but built and very intense. He pulled me aside one day and said, "Ted, I believe you can go out and earn six figures your first year of business."

At this time of my life, it wasn't about the money. I just looked up to him. I wanted my boss' approval. So, I put my head down and went after the goal for 12 straight months. By the last month of the year, I cracked a six-figures income in the insurance business.

When I got the news, I partied hard. I overdosed and ended up on my kitchen floor at four in the morning, out of my mind off a bag of cocaine, two ecstasy pills, and 15 drinks of alcohol. I could feel my soul leaving my body. I looked up into my brother's eyes, gasping for breath, thinking, "This is it."

As this was happening, I had this shameful feeling. I wondered, "What will my parents think? Their son dying of an overdose on his kitchen floor—and what an awful way to go."

It's funny how things turned out that way. You would think at that moment I'd be like, "I want to save myself! I want to hold onto my life." But all I felt was intense shame.

Everything went black. Soon after, I was miraculously revived. When I woke up, I realized I had a second chance.

Obviously, the money hadn't done it for me. It didn't fulfill me, so I grabbed onto the next big thing. I thought, "Maybe if I make partner, and I get to management, my life will change. I will get power. I will be respected. I will have status. Maybe that's the answer!"

So, I put my head down and worked hard again for six or seven years. I went after it even harder than before. I grinded it out for 17, sometimes 18 hours a day; whatever it took, I did it. By now, I was 28.

Then the big day comes to reap my reward. I'm standing on the top floor of the SunTrust Building in Orlando, Florida, and I'm waiting to hear if all my efforts paid off. It's finally the day when I'm going to find out if I became one of the top partners in the company. My assistant walks through the doors. She's got this yellow envelope and she says, "I got the news!"

She smiles as she hands it to me. I open it up and read the words: *Ted McGrath. Number 5 partner out of 500 for the #1 life insurance company in the country.*

I felt a burst of excitement but once the butterflies settled, I was left with this question: *"Is this really all there is to my life? Is this really what I worked seven years for?"*

I didn't like the answers to those questions so I walked into the office down the hall, turned in my resignation letter, and never returned.

After that, I thought, "Okay. I got it now. That wasn't the answer. I know what I'll do. I'll become an entrepreneur."

With this goal in mind, I moved all the way across the country, from Florida to California in a $100,000 car. I bought a million-dollar condo, and started two businesses.

Cut to two years later. I'm sitting on my couch with my face in my hands. My businesses are failing because I lack passion about what I am doing. Below me on the street a truck is towing my vehicle out of the driveway. My third foreclosure notice sits on the table next to piles and piles of bills. I can't help wondering: "What the hell am I'm going to do with my life? I have barely any money left."

This moment of reflection forced me to realize that not only did life in New York not fulfill me, but money didn't either. Trying to assess where things went wrong, I thought back to when I was six and learned my parents were getting a divorce. The message I got was, "You're not lovable. You're not good enough."

That's the burden I carried around all these years. But I wasn't right. I saw for the first time my parents *did* care about me. All the struggling to achieve I had been doing wasn't bringing them closer—it was actually pushing them and everyone else further away.

I fell down to my knees. I sobbed as all the years of built-up feelings of unworthiness slid off my shoulders. And as I stood back up, an incredible rush of energy surged inside of me. I decided right then that I wanted to do something to make a difference. I wanted to do something I felt passionate about. Something I loved. Something I had always wanted to do.

Reviewing my life, I realized that when I was in the insurance business, I encountered coaching programs that interested me but I never followed my passion. I never pursued it. For the first time, I realized I wanted to be a coach. I wanted to help other people struggling to find their own purpose and meaning.

That day I started writing down all the things I had learned so far, and what I realized is, I had all this knowledge. I had learned a lot about sales. I had also possessed leadership skills from directing a group of over 60 salespeople.

It's interesting, though, that while the product I sold was insurance packages, my product was never myself.

My product was never:

- *What do I know?*
- *Who am I?*
- *What's unique about me in the world?*
- *How do I serve others?*

> *It was the first time I was doing something I was really passionate about, something that was creative and entirely mine.*

But what if it could be?

Seven days later, I met with my first client. I still remember shaking from nervousness. I had never been paid for my personal gifts before. Instead, I had been always paid by the insurance company for selling their product. At the end of the session, I asked for my fee. Though the amount was much less than what I what I was used to making, it was the most meaningful check I had ever received.

After that first experience, it got easier. I got the next client, and the one after that. I worked as hard as I did before, but it was different this time. It was the first time I was doing something I was really passionate about, something that was creative and entirely mine.

Parents and children of divorce can learn from separation

My personal story revolves around the issue of not feeling connection and love. When we are young, we tend to make up stories in our heads that feel real to us at the time, and help us make sense of the world around us. However, they might not actually reflect reality. For example, as observant adults, we come to realize that our parents weren't perfect. They were just trying their best. This realization helped me to look at the great things my parents *did* do.

Most parents just want better relationships with their kids.

Oftentimes, all they need to do is communicate more directly. Unfortunately, lots of people never do so, because confronting the real problem seems too difficult. It doesn't have to be so

> Sometimes, all you have to do to start a conversation is ask, *"How are you feeling?"*

complicated though. Sometimes, all you have to do to start a conversation is ask, *"How are you feeling?"*

If I was asked that, and felt like I could say what was on my mind, it would have saved me years of misdirected thinking.

Kids need to be asked this, but aren't. Parents need to guide the communication and say: *"How are you feeling? Is there anything you want to say to your mom or dad?"*

I don't think that happens as much as it should.

When you take responsibility for your mistakes, you gain personal power

When I came out to California before I began coaching, I was in a transitional phase. I had stopped doing drugs for quite some time, but I continued to compulsively drink. I wanted to fully commit to becoming a coach and speaker, but I wasn't yet the person I wanted to be. I struggled with my identity.

It was a dark time. I would go out and meet with girls, but I was never in an honest, committed relationship. Deep down inside, I knew I had something special to give, but I didn't know how to meet somebody the right way. I was lonely and would get really drunk and at two or three in the morning end up across the border with a new girl.

I remember one of my darkest moments. I had just gotten back at seven in the morning, after I had been with someone, then thought about how I had to lead a seminar the following Monday. I came into that space thinking, "Man, my whole life is a lie. I want to be great but look at who I am." I knew I had to change. And I did.

> "Man, my whole life is a lie. I want to be great but look at who I am."

Slowly, I started to repair my life. I've always been a searcher of spirituality, and I started to find more meaningful processes until I turned my life around and cleaned up. And, man, I cleaned up big time! The moment I realized I had made real progress is when I got into a solid relationship. I have been dating my girlfriend for almost three years now. I know she's the person I'm going to marry. She's the best thing that has ever happened to me.

Be the person you know you can be

I knew that in order to successfully coach, I needed to become the person I always envisioned. For me, that individual was somebody who didn't go out and drink. It's not that I have an issue with somebody who drinks alcohol, but I didn't like the person I was when I was doing that.

Take responsibility for your actions. Always look in the mirror, and reflect on who you are and what you're doing. Once I was able to be honest with myself, I was able to be honest with others. That changed it for me. Nowadays, my girlfriend and I can talk about anything. She knows my past. She knows it all. That's the greatest place to be in life: where there's nothing to hide. And for the first time, I feel really seen and loved.

Education as a means to help others

I want to help people who are addicted to drugs. Coming from a place of understanding, I'm not going place blame or simply say, "Don't do drugs."

I choose to raise awareness through education by supporting the largest non-governmental program on drugs called, "Truth About Drugs." I spread awareness at my seminars and in sessions with clients.

The whole purpose of the "Truth about Drugs" campaign is education. I've made so many decisions in my life based on misinformation, I know if other people are given honest information they can arrive at the right decision for themselves.

(*You can visit DrugFreeWorld.org for more information about this amazing organization.*)

Finding Your Own Voice

One of my flagship brands is 'Message to Millions.'

The first thing we do is educate entrepreneurs. "You have a message to share," is the message. From the stage, I let them know they have a unique life story to tell and important lessons to teach.

It's important to know that when you find your life story, you find your message and your purpose. For instance, a potential health coach may suddenly realize, "I healed myself through this process. Now, I want to help others in the same way." Similarly, someone wishing to be a life coach may discover, "I have these tools in my life that have helped my relationships. Now, I want to pass them on."

My job is to help clients understand their story, their message, and their system so they can go and teach others. Once this is in place, I help them develop a process to get paid. I actually help people become one-on-one coaches and international speakers. I aid them in establishing their online programs.

Some people find us on the web and go through our video programs. Others attend an in-person four-day seminar. We literally have people fly across the world. They come from all different countries like Nigeria, France, Switzerland, and Africa.

It's amazing when someone can share their truth and impact others. Today, more than ever, people need to have a connection to your brand, no matter what it is. When they do, they gain a vital connection from hearing another human being's story. Ultimately, when somebody understands themselves better, they become equipped to make better life decisions because they have more confidence and trust. Helping to foster this awakening is so important in my work.

Why 'the struggle makes you stronger' is misleading

I think it's inaccurate when I hear people say this. If people truly operated from their fullest potential, would we really be in a world where people turn to drugs? Would we really be in a world where people cheat in their relationships? Would we really be in a world where people act unethically in business?

If people were not struggling so hard, just trying so hard to exist, then they would wake up each morning saying, "Wow, I'm going to go create beauty and magnificence today! I'm going to go without stopping."

Now, that would be a hell of a world.

Have a mission in life

I've heard people say, "Have a mission in life. Get a cause. Then life will be great." Well, there are layers to this idea. I believe a person must have a purpose and serve it in the best and biggest way possible. It's important that your gifts are on a level that is meaningful, personal, ethical, and serves a greater good.

You should devote your life to getting the tools you need to become more powerful, to become more passionate, and to become more connected to the people you love. You should especially serve those people who cannot serve themselves. That's a great life and that's what I'm doing every single day.

It's important that your gifts are on a level that is meaningful, personal, ethical, and serves a greater good.

Chapter 6

"You Are Your Own Job Security"

A conversation with Jim Fitzpatrick, Owner of San Diego Magazine & Former Owner of Entrepreneur Magazine

How Jim got into the publishing business

In the mid-1980's, there was no magazine for small businesses. There was *Fortune* and *Businessweek* for large companies, and *Venture* for midsized companies, but 90 percent of all businesses in America were small businesses and there was no publication for them. I recognized that niche and saw that if *Entrepreneur Magazine* was cleaned up and made into a real magazine, it could do very well since there was a big market.

Jim Fitzpatrick

None of my business partners knew anything about publishing, but it seemed like a good idea at the time. Back then, not many people even knew what the word, 'entrepreneur' meant if you can believe it. In fact, whenever I went on sales calls, I had to spell the name out.

Things have changed quite a bit since then.

Take risks

If it's a good idea, try it and see what happens. I was a pilot in the Air Force, and there were many times when I was definitely afraid; scared stiff in fact. But I learned a long time ago that fear is just an emotion. It's like a door.

You can let fear stop you from opening that door, or you can open it and go right through. I've found that most of the time, once you pass through that door of fear, you can look back and see it wasn't so bad after all. You've made it.

Have a deep talk with yourself. Ask:

- *How badly do I want this?*
- *Do I want it bad enough to face my fear?*
- *Is my desire strong enough to put the fear aside?*

Because that's what you have to do. You need to push doubt away and go with your plan. It's like the Nike slogan, determine what you need to do and *just do it.*

Go to college

I went to Valparaiso University, an extremely good school in northern Indiana where I received a great education. While I was in the Air Force, I also went to night school and earned an MBA from Golden Gate University. It's not like I was actively using a lot of what I learned in school, but I learned *how to learn.* I learned how to evaluate situations, and make decisions and that's what's really important.

I highly recommend college to young people. Having a degree was the ticket to obtaining good jobs in the marketplace. From there, I got the opportunity to start my own business. For those of you struggling with the daunting costs of higher education, it's important to know there are many opportunities to obtain scholarships, grant aids, and low-interest loans.

Also, take the time to ensure you are making a good decision on what school to attend. Your question should be two-fold: are you going to get a good education in the area you wish to pursue? And if you cannot afford college without going into extreme debt, are there collegiate alternatives?

Big, common mistakes young entrepreneurs can easily avoid

The number one mistake is not having enough capital. This is the biggest cause of failure - you don't have enough money to operate your business. Learn how to do a business plan, then make sure that you have enough money to survive at least a three-year period within your plan.

Another common mistake: people don't do enough homework. There's no excuse for that when there is so much information available online today. You can research your topic of interest to be sure you are creating a product with a real need.

I frequently see this mistake in the publishing industry. For instance, I encounter individuals who think they have a great idea but that's just not commercially viable. I always use this analogy. Someone approaches me saying: "I like horses. You like horses. *Everybody likes horses*, so I think I'll start a magazine about horses. Folks will love it!"

Slow down. Nowadays, it's easy to start a business, especially a magazine. With the help of a computer, you can design your magazine, take it to a printer, and you've already got a publication. But is there really a market for your horse magazine? Ask yourself, *Who is going to read it? Who's going to advertise in this magazine?* You may have a great idea, but you must fulfill a real need.

> You may have a great idea, but you must fulfill a real need.

Build a good team

You can't do it all alone. The people you hire will make you successful, so know exactly what you're looking for in your team. I had two completely different teams spanning my two periods of publishing. From 1994 to 2005, we had more of a typical publishing staff: writers, editors, designers, etc. Everybody did their own thing. My second time around in 2010, the whole media world had changed.

Digital media was everything, so I needed people who were both journalists and digital media experts.

The best part about entrepreneurship

Freedom. Entrepreneurship requires responsibility but there's a reward in knowing you built something, either a business or a product that people want. That's what's most fulfilling.

Embrace change

A media company doesn't survive long without adapting to the changing needs of the market. My first time around with *San Diego Magazine*, luxury products/ services were our niche. We had to market our publication to a very high-end, older demographic who could afford such expensive products.

Ever since the 2008 crash, the luxury market has declined. Nowadays, our advertisers wish to target millennials. To reach this younger generation I had to know what millennials wanted, so I put a new team together. That's how we changed *San Diego Magazine* to reflect the new reality.

Our content keeps up with the times too. *Hatch* is our new business magazine about innovation in San Diego and it has been extremely well-received.

There are three major innovation hubs in the world. One is Silicon Valley, another is Boston, but the third and maybe biggest is actually San Diego--a fact that no one seems to know.

Residents in San Diego don't even know what's going on!

When we found out what was happening in our own backyard, we decided to create a tech magazine that was different. That's the key to this market. You have to stay innovative.

What happens when older people refuse to embrace the digital revolution

You become a dinosaur. You get left behind. Just look at how people consume media now. They don't read the paper. They find out the news on Twitter as it unfolds. By the time a story is broadcast on television or appears in a weekly magazine, it's old news. In our business, we must stay one step ahead of the game. We have to be involved. We have to know everything.

Worst entrepreneurial moment

When I first acquired *San Diego Magazine,* I did a lot of research. I wrote a business plan and felt pretty confident. But in our second year of operation, something happened that I didn't plan for. Paper prices skyrocketed. Not only that, they doubled. And that's one of the biggest expenses we have in magazine publishing.

That unforeseen development threw my business plan out the window. I had to make adjustments. I learned something extremely valuable in the process. You can plan all you want but you must be flexible. You have to be nimble and ready to make adjustments at any point.

The definition of a meaningful life

The answer is very personal and very different for everybody. For me it's, what have I done to make a difference in somebody else's life?

One of the great things about the publishing industry is we really do affect people's lives every day. Each time a consumer picks up the magazine and reads it, they learn about something they didn't know anything about before. They experience something they otherwise wouldn't have had, had they not seen it in our magazine.

On the personal side, what matters most is my great family: three kids and six grandkids. They're all fantastic, wonderfully successful, and happy people.

So, when I think of a meaningful life, it's all about enjoying every chapter. I've had a lot of different chapters to look back on and I truly enjoyed every single one of them.

Advice to the new generation:

Do what you enjoy. It's so important to get out of bed every day and say, "I want to go do this. I *want* to go to work."

Whether you're a carpenter, a publisher, a doctor, or a lawyer, make it count. Life is too short not to like what you do.

There is no such thing as job security

When I first got out of college, it was a different time. People would go to work for big corporations. This was different than what my parents did, where their generation just stayed with the same company for 30 years. When I was in the military, men continued in the services as a career for 20 years because there was job security.

I learned something different in the military. There's no such thing as security.

You are your own security.

You are your own job security.

You have to rely on yourself and your own abilities. The old concept of job security doesn't exist any longer. Don't count on pensions or retirement. It's gone. There's no one who can give you security other than yourself.

Finding the confidence to bet on himself

I learned self-reliance in the Air Force. I had the opportunity to do some amazing things as a pilot and learned very quickly that if I can do this, I can do anything.

Inspiration

I like to take on new challenges to see how far I can go and what I can do. I make sure I'm always doing my best. For *San Diego Magazine*, the philosophy is whatever we do must be high-quality. We set the bar high because we find a challenge inspiring.

The student becomes the mentor

It's important for the older generation (like myself) to listen to the younger generation. Young people have many good ideas and thoughts that aren't tainted by years of experience. This is a blessing as it tends to make them much more creative.

I have an office full of millennials and I love them because of their high energy. They're very smart. They want ownership. It is very important for entrepreneurs to understand that when you create an organization, you really have to give people ownership of something and let them do it.

The millennials we've been fortunate enough to have on our team are like that. For example, we have a very large events program. We do 16 events per year. I tell our team, "These are the events that you're assigned. I want you to own the event and run it like it's your own business."

The great thing is they don't need to be micromanaged. They just run with any project and make it their own.

The worst mistake you can make in life

I think the worst thing you can do is not learn. I know I am ignorant in some areas, and when I am, I say, "Teach me!"

> *I think the worst thing you can do is not learn. I know I am ignorant in some areas, and when I am, I say, "Teach me!"*

Speaking of learning, one of my closest late friends was Saul Price, the founder of Price Club, now Costco. Saul was a brilliant man and an entrepreneur all his life. I had the opportunity to meet with him frequently and one time I asked, "Saul, why do I have to learn like this? Why can't you just give me an injection of your experience?"

He said to me, "Jim, it just doesn't work that way. You learn by your own experience."

The future looks bright

I am very optimistic about the future. I know there's tremendous potential. I truly believe the younger generation can fix what we messed up because they're a lot smarter than we are and more creative. Today everything requires a lot of creativity and you have to be quick on your feet. So, I have a lot of confidence in their potential.

How Jim hopes to be remembered

As somebody who did their very best they could with what they had. That's really it. I had a good life, a good time, and I did my best to do my best.

Chapter 7

Don't Wait. Take Your Own Path and Follow It

An Interview with Mark Shockley, an Innovative Hollywood Producer

Mark owns not one, but two successful entertainment companies

I have a lot of energy and Los Angeles is a very ambitious town. To stay here and be part of the game, two companies are better than one. Evolution LA is a service-based company. We promote movies mostly, but also big brands, like Coca Cola's NOS Energy Drink.

Some of our film campaigns include:

- Mission Impossible: Rogue Nation
- Transformers: Age of Extinction
- Ice Age
- Rio
- Gone Girl
- Life of Pi
- The Wolf of Wall Street and
- Avengers Alliance

Our goal is to get butts into seats. We started in 2006 with Borat. It was the first time "going viral" had driven movie ticket sales. Sacha Baron Cohen and his team were so brilliant. They really knew how to work it.

From my work in entertainment, I realized the importance of intellectual property and licensing. My wife was an animal trainer, and I used to help her, leading to my idea for a company called 'Green Screen Animals.'

We offer stock footage of exotic and domestic animals we license to filmmakers and storytellers. Some of our collection includes alligators, baboons, bears, bearded dragons, cheetahs, coyotes, elephants, leopards, lions, octopi, penguins, reindeer, scorpions, snakes, tigers, ands zebras.

I run both companies out of our Santa Monica, California location.

These businesses are a combination of my two passions. I'm passionate about animals and production, so we decided to merge the two. Because of my history in these fields, I can speak the trainer language a little better than most, and help with the studios, as well as corporate clients, and ad agencies.

Mark struggled for years to make it in Hollywood

I had kids, so I had to moonlight. I worked as an editor at night. During the day, I would work from 9 am to 6 pm. I would get to hang out with my young son from 6 pm to 9 pm. I would put him to bed, then I would go back to work and edit from 10 pm to 2 am. I did this schedule for two years, surviving on double Starbucks shots. I burned the candle, and only slept five hours per night. I had to do it because I needed that extra revenue.

L.A. is a hard place to survive in. Just moving here from New York, figuring out the industry, and ultimately providing a living for my family is an accomplishment. Being able to buy a home and pay for school can be challenging. It can be really expensive. Anyone that's done this, knows how difficult it is. You have to really work hard to become and stay successful. I established a couple of businesses I'm really proud of and feel like I've finally won.

Never stop innovating

I've paid my dues. You can't rest on your laurels because there's always somebody coming up, who is twice as talented as you, and waiting for your spot.

Innovation is everything. If you don't improve, you'll be passed by.

> *Innovation is everything. If you don't improve, you'll be passed by.*

I've seen the industry change and I continually ask myself how I can grow with it. This is the question we must ask ourselves all the time to stay relevant.

I value the younger players because I watch what's happening to them. How are they consuming media? Look at my son. He can watch a YouTube video on a 70-inch plasma and then catch a feature on his phone. So, I take my cues from that.

Entrepreneurship wasn't a choice. It was a necessity!

I always had a problem with authority. I don't like to be told what to do and I couldn't work for anybody else. I have a laundry list of jobs that didn't work out, and I learned quite young that I needed to make my own way. I would rather work quietly on my own in some corner than work for somebody else.

Walk the talk

I used to be great at starting things, but never finished them. I eventually realized my problem was fear of failure. Hard work means buckling down and doing what you need to do. Identify your priorities and follow them through to the end. I know so many people with great ideas, but unless you are willing to do the hard work to get them done, they go nowhere.

Dark moments in my career

When the housing crash happened in 2009, things slowed down dramatically. It was nerve-racking. I remember waking up at three in the morning in a panic. I rode my bike from Venice where I live, to Malibu in the dark.

The whole time I was pedaling, I kept thinking of ways to save my business, to stop myself from defaulting on my house. That's the kind of working without a net that's required when you're an entrepreneur. Sometimes your back is against the wall and there's no one to save you. This is what drives you. I had no alternative, so I had to make it through. And that's what builds character.

Higher education - to go or not go to college

I don't think college is for everyone. It's a mistake to force your kid to go. It's one thing if they want to, or if they need a little support, but let them decide.

School was a big struggle for me. I was the typical ADD poster boy and the learning curves were too much with my dyslexia. I knew I wasn't stupid, it just wasn't for me. I went to college and studied journalism for two years but never graduated. Leaving college was the best decision I ever made. I felt completely liberated because I didn't fit within that structure.

Carve out your own education path

Classroom learning wasn't my thing, but I always put a priority on learning. Whether it's on-the-job training, or through experience, I learn by doing.

Advice for the next generation

Your emphasis needs to be understanding the problems associated with environmental changes. Are we going to save our planet? I don't see how a job in the future can avoid facing this because we are getting to the tipping point.

On a personal level, don't follow the money. Follow what brings you joy and the money will come. Follow your heart, not your head. That's the most important thing. Don't wait.

Take your own path and follow it. You can't let anyone else be responsible for your life. You must go out and make it for yourself.

How to break into the entertainment business

Be pro-active. You can earn a lot of money by making someone else's life easier. If you're not an entrepreneur yet—if you're working for someone else, still treat their company like it's your own. Think of ways you can help it perform better. Ask only the questions you need to know. Figure the rest out on your own.

As an employer, I meet many people coming out of film school showing promise, but when I interview them, they don't know what they want to do. It makes me think, "Couldn't you have at least lied?" Seriously.

If you're applying for a job, act like the job you are applying for is the job you want. I don't need to hear you are still searching for other positions. Pretend like the job you are applying for is the cat's meow and you really want it.

Carpe Diem

Try your best. We all know someone who screwed up an opportunity. If you stick around long enough in the entertainment industry, you are going to be given a chance. It's up to you to be ready.

I got an opportunity through MGM. At the time, I was doing pro-bono work for Catholic charities. I loved working. I loved shooting. I loved the human stories. I loved editing. I was doing a piece on homelessness and the Good Shepherd Center aiding homeless mothers.

This video ended up in the hands of my wife who gave it to her boss. He liked what he saw so much he gave me an opportunity.

Of course, you could say, "Your wife worked at MGM, so she got you the job." But the truth is she really just got me the opportunity. When given the chance to do that first video for them, I could have screwed off, but I didn't. I put a lot of time into it. I focused. That effort led to another job, and that one led to another job, which led to another job.

What matters most

Evolution LA has worked with a lot of high-profile celebrities. I have personally interviewed a good majority of them.

Hugh Jackman from the X-men franchise is such a gentleman with amazing talent. Sacha Baron Cohen is a creative genius. There are others: Carol Burnett, Dustin Hoffman, Jim Carrey, Jennifer Lopez, Bruno Mars, the list really goes on.

These are people who have set the bar high, who have put so many things in motion. We've been blessed to work with them and it's been really, really fun.

But I only pinch myself when I look at my family because that's where it's at for me. When I'm with my Mom or friends back East, they may say things like, "No way, man! You got to work with that person!" At those times, I'm more aware of what's going on, but I don't dwell on those experiences. That's not my thing.

Being a good parent is what's most important to me. That's all I care about. With any accomplishment, it's more about my family and my kids. I want to be respected and loved by them. That's what I truly value.

Don't be intimidated by other people, even celebrities

I always try to stay humble and just be of service to each project and my creative partners. I let the work itself dictate what I do.

One of the most important things to realize is that each person puts on their pants everyday just like you do. Even if we have different wants and needs, we all have the same core.

Even if someone is wealthy or famous, it doesn't mean they can't have a bad day. Or that they don't have challenges in their own lives. Celebrities are regular people too. The more you walk with your own power and your own knowledge—the more you proceed with confidence—the better off you will be.

The joy of creativity and vision

I love having a vision and making it happen. It's fulfilling for me. One day, I had this idea for Green Screen Animals. I pitched it to my friend and he said, "Hey, I like that idea. I'll be your partner for this amount of money." So, we went out, got investors, and just made it happen. Now something exists where nothing did before.

Mark's philosophy

Stay at it. Dust yourself off and keep going. There have been many times I've had to make tough choices. When that happens, you just have to pull your hood up and walk into the wind. You have to hunker down and move through it. You have no choice.

When you make a mistake, make amends, and move on. Let it go. Every day is an opportunity to reset. So just reset and keep going.

Chapter 8

If you are doing the right thing, success will come to you.

An Interview with Ken Kerry, Direct Marketer and Co-owner of Script to Screen

Ever seen an infomercial? Then, you've probably witnessed Ken's work

Script to Screen is an integrated, performance-marketing agency. We spend our client's ad budget on commercials, digital marketing content, or social media campaigns, giving them an immediate Return on Investment (ROI) (hence the name "direct marketing").

We call ourselves the "results agency," and have developed winning campaigns for multi million dollar brands, like

Ken Kerry

Keurig, Nescafé, Health Master, Bare Minerals, and more. We create content for individuals and companies, then promote and sell their products to give them a rapid ROI.

What we do differs from other marketers. Our content appears in the TV, radio, and digital space, so our advertisements can be anywhere and everywhere. With us, you don't continually pay for our services. Our model is this: if you give us X dollars, you will get X dollars back. The efficiency ratio is quick.

Ken's career began in college when he turned a sports scholarship into a marketing opportunity

San Diego State gave me a scholarship to play football, but I selfishly took it to attend their renowned Television Journalism program. I mostly kept to my studies, but my knowledge of football helped me direct sports games for broadcast. Here I learned the most important thing about television. Even it's a sports game, you must tell a story. With event coverage, the story must include whatever is unfolding live and you have to figure out the best way to communicate it.

Straight out of college, I was hired as a production assistant at a network, which is basically a glorified name for a coffee-runner. But I was around the people I needed to be around. Remember, if you ever have the opportunity of being around the right people, take it. Then do your job and keep your ears wide open. Absorb everything. Keep absorbing until you get an idea of what everyone is doing. This will teach you what you need to know.

At 22, I was working making $50 a day. Yes, the pay was low, but I loved it. I was surrounded by the bustling energy required for a live TV production. I was gaining valuable new knowledge every day. I even met my wife, Barbi, there (she almost didn't talk to me at first because of our uncanny name pairing.) I worked there for seven years and even covered the Olympics which was a dream of mine, but I still wanted to direct sports games. Unfortunately, this was before ESPN and cable. For me to get a director job at the network, someone had to quit or pass away. I calculated it would be 30 or 40 years until I had my shot.

Barbi also had bigger aspirations than working for a network and interviewing sports people all her life. While dating, we both became disenchanted with the industry. We wanted to do more.

Ken and Barbi knew they could be more honest marketers

Barbi and I watched a lot of TV commercials featuring what we saw as "snake oil salesmen" being sleazy. Although I had respect for their success, I didn't like how they achieved it. We thought we could do that better. So, we gave it a shot.

Extra motivation was close to home

One of my biggest life mentors is my father-in-law. He is an amazing human being who drops wisdom left and right. If you put your head down, and listen for just a minute, you will learn something. He always gives positive words of advice; read this book, do that, absorb this. He says most of us don't recognize the beauty of what we are doing today. Because of the household I grew up in, this kind of positivity was new and refreshing.

I lost my father when I was a senior in high school. I never felt I had a positive male role model because even before he died, my father struggled with his own demons. Meanwhile, my mother worked a 24-hour shift as a nurse, so we rarely saw her, but she did all she could to keep the household together.

She made sure we kept out of trouble, and moved us into good neighborhoods.

When I met my future father-in-law, I thought *wow!* He had such a genuine interest in getting to know me, as a person, and he made a big impact on my life. Not a lot of people were positive like him. Barbi and I thought he was something special, that we could harness that positivity and sell motivation tapes featuring him as the speaker. After appealing to the right investors, including my father-in-law, we received the finances to make our first infomercial. Using our insider knowledge of television, journalism, and writing, we created something we liked and put it on air.

In reality, we knew nothing. Yes, we knew we had something special, but we didn't know how to create or market it correctly. As entrepreneurs, we had to figure out how to make our infomercial product, how to write the script and produce it independently. The two of us were the mailing department, the customer department—everything. We left our jobs, and invested our whole lives in our ad. Then it bombed.

Leaving a successful job to pursue something entirely different, and then failing at it, was a smack in the gut. But Barbi and I thought that we had to do something to make this situation right. There were investors, family, and money involved (and by the way, it's hard to go to Thanksgiving and look your family investors in the eye when you've lost their money).

We didn't want to be indebted to anyone, nor did we want to be seen as screw-ups. We kept pushing, dissecting other infomercials, and working days and nights to analyze what we were doing right, and where we were falling short.

What we realized is an infomercial equals a commercial plus information. We had been informing more than we were selling. So, we learned how to sell *and* give value. For example, out of total naivety, we put credits at the end of our infomercial like a TV show. We didn't even know you're not supposed to do that for a commercial. But we learned from it and then put our mistakes behind us.

Script to Screen's origins

We received a call one day from the director of a company called Life Sign. He said he wanted to pay us to do an infomercial. Back then, it was just me and Barbi working in a small office. I put my hand over the phone and said I needed to consult with our "marketing department." In reality, I yelled over to Barbi that we had our first client.

Life Sign offered a gradual smoking cessation program. E.D Marshall and Florence Henderson (from the *Brady Bunch*) were the spokespeople. Both ex-smokers, they wanted to help others quit. We liked that. We wanted to help other people too. The infomercial was successful and cemented our growing reputation in our industry.

Another one of our first clients was "Hooked On Phonics," a program designed to help people learn to read. We believed in the product, and recognized the best way to sell was to have the actual people it helped speak on camera about the way it transformed their lives. Our approach worked and enabled the company to sell millions of dollars' worth of products.

The hardest thing Ken has ever had to face

Barbi is not only my business partner, but my partner in life and my best friend. For over 30 years, we've been able to do what we love together. Then one day when our business was booming, and the company was really clicking, we received a phone call. The doctor told us that Barbi had cancer.

I had a duty to all of my employees, but I also had a moral obligation to my wife and our young daughter. The hardest thing was getting that phone call and being unsure what tomorrow would look like. Barbi was diagnosed with breast cancer at the height of our company's success. When you wake up in the morning, and see the woman you love throwing up in a bowl, whatever you have to do the rest of the day suddenly becomes irrelevant. What mattered most was helping her get through it and being there for my daughter.

While we thought about the different directions this news could take our personal lives, we also had to be practical. How might it affect our business? What could I do to keep the company going, yet remain considerate of our employees? After all, they had families too and were depending on us.

Tragedies happen. It's how you deal with them that matters. You really must examine the situation and make the best decision based on the information you have at the time. If you play the "could have, should have" game, you will only wear yourself out as well as others around you.

Instead you have to work, then move forward, because things can change at any time. When it came to Barbi's illness, we had to make decisions on an hourly basis. Do we focus on the client or Barbi's chemo? Barbi could be scheduled to be in the hospital at 3pm on Tuesday, yet I had a business meeting at 2 pm. Should I reschedule or cancel? What do I do in that situation? I had to juggle both the personal and the professional. Did I always get it right? I hope so. I had to make the best decision at the time. In that case, I left the meeting by 2:30 to be with her.

In terms of our employees, we were fortunate that our business was family-oriented. We have an amazing group of people we've been working with for years. When building a company, I advise that you understand your employees on a personal level before knowing them on a professional level. There are some great experts out there, but they may not align with you personally and ethically. Because we built our company with people we liked and trusted, we created a solid foundation. And when I said I had to leave by 2:30, they all understood--because not only did I know them, they knew me, and they knew my family.

Ken loves his clients

We did a lot of work in the golf and tennis world before we met Barney Adams. Like us, Adams was an entrepreneur. He had just developed a unique golf club and wanted to make an infomercial about it.

Adams believed, with all his heart, in his product and was willing to bet everything he had on it. Because of that, he packed up his car (a beat-up 1974 Cadillac) and drove from Texas to California with his trunk full of golf clubs. This was Barney's dream. When someone comes to you like this, when someone says to you, "This is my whole life," it can be a burden or an opportunity. We saw it as an opportunity.

We told him, "We may not have all the answers, but we have a lot of experience to give you the best chance to succeed." Instead of asking for a certain amount of money, we invested in the project and it turned out to be a profitable decision— personally and professionally.

Within a year, Barney had sold enough golf clubs to shake the golf industry to its foundation. Not only that, I had made a new friend that I still have today.

The best part of being an entrepreneur

The best part is just living an exciting life. Nothing is guaranteed. If you like challenges, being an entrepreneur is the best way to be challenged on a daily basis. When people complain about their problems, I remind them it's another chance to succeed. It's always exciting to find new solutions to problems.

Plus, I can go surfing whenever I want.

What it means to have vision

Having a vision can be a lonely place. But to me, a vision also means doing the best you can when foreseeing the world's direction. You will have an indicator here or there, and you need to try to predict where it will go.

The other day, someone told me our company is one of the last ones standing in the direct-response industry. It's because we've never stopped innovating. For instance, there's no question that media has changed. For our company to stay relevant, we needed to evolve with it from record tapes to CDs, from video on demand to streaming, we always needed to anticipate the next evolutionary phase to keep growing.

You must innovate, or you will die. In the 1920s, there was a national leather company that made seats for horse-drawn wagons. Then, a guy named Ford came along and started making cars. The leather-body company didn't innovate new products to compete, so the company died. Innovation is absolutely critical.

You must innovate, or you will die.

You don't have to lose the core of what you're doing, but you must adapt to changing conditions. You can either run for the bus or wait for it to get there. There's nothing wrong with having visions, but you have to keep them under your control.

You also can't accomplish a vision alone, so it's important to have more than just one person understanding your strategy. For example, in our small industry, our vision included taking content and creating value by distributing it on different platforms. People gather information differently today; they can Google whatever they want at any time.

Whether it's for a CEO of a multibillion-dollar corporation or a small business owner, we have to keep the store open all the time. We can market it correctly and put it in the right places, and then we can increase your business 10 times over. Is what we do labor intensive? Yes. Does it take a lot of mental skill? Yes. That's the price of business.

> If you can communicate effectively, you will go further than you ever thought.

Ken's version of skipping a step

The biggest mistake entrepreneurs make is thinking it will cost them less time and money to do it on their own. If you are going to grab 50 percent of people instead of 20 percent, your runway needs to be bigger, and it may cost more.

I don't think people should jump or take "leaps" of faith into anything. Skipping a step can even be counterproductive if you move too fast. Instead, skipping a step means learning something in-between.

This means getting as much information as you can while you grow—to support that gut feeling attached to your vision.

The most important skill you need to have as an entrepreneur

Hands down, it's effective written and verbal communication. One time we were on set, burning 20 to 30 thousand dollars an hour. We needed to make a shift in a time slot to accommodate the celebrity we had that day. That meant we had to write new lines for them, but our official writer wasn't on set.

I asked an employee with effective communication skills, "Can you write us out of this mess?" She said yes, and pulled it off. Her ability to communicate well saved us hundreds of thousands of dollars, as well as our credibility.

As an entrepreneur, you must learn how to communicate at a moment's notice. I always tell people in college to learn how to write and to speak, because if you can communicate effectively, you will go further than you ever thought.

Find meaning in your life by impacting others

A while ago, we developed a deep relationship with a valued client. We took the client from $100 million to $100 billion in one year. About five years into the relationship, the CEO decided to fire us and go in-house with their marketing. Not only that, they scooped up some of my best employees and asked them to go work for them.

Did this hurt? Hell, yes it did. But there was little I could do about it. I couldn't offer my employees the same benefits our former client was offering. Still, I put my ego aside, and told my team members I would support them and the transition.

Two years later, I happened to talk to some of these individuals. They told me the move greatly improved their and their family's lives. Despite everything, I was happy by that. The truth was I couldn't compete financially with this former client. I am glad they did what was best for them and for my previous employees.

With anything in life, the best thing to do is try to be honest. Ask yourself, are you impacting people's lives? If so, is it for good or bad? Always try to do good by others.

I feel my life is meaningful because others have affirmed that I have touched their lives in positive ways. This knowledge brings meaning and purpose to my existence.

Be a dreamer *and* a doer

You should truly explore what you want to do in your life, not only dream about it. My daughter says, "Don't wish that you want to do something. Just get up and do it." Fear will stop you every single time, if you let it.

Look. If you know in your heart that you are going to affect people positively, then make it happen. Believe in yourself, and then do what you need to do. I wouldn't necessarily call it karma, but if you are doing the right thing, success will come to you. It will manifest somewhere, somehow, and someday.

Chapter 9

My Currency is Adventure

An interview with Jessica Jackley, Co-founder of Kiva.org

Kiva has been able to reframe stories of poverty into stories of entrepreneurship.

The perfect investment

Growing up, I always wanted to be helpful. I already knew I was one of the luckiest people in the world. I was blessed with a wonderful family and had everything I needed. I dabbled in various courses and jobs until I heard a transformational lecture at Stanford University by Dr. Muhammad Yunus. He's the Nobel Peace Prize–winning founder of the Grameen Bank, which has provided microfinancing to more than eight million borrowers, mostly desperately poor women with no collateral.

When Dr. Yunus discussed microfinance, it resonated deeply. This epiphany led me to quit my job at Stanford, and take an unpaid internship in East Africa, where I heard stories from people who received grants to start or grow tiny businesses.

Working directly with people living in poverty and hearing their stories of strength and dignity, rather than stories focused on sadness and suffering was my big moment.

I discovered interesting, smart, and hardworking people who just needed access to capital to get started. I felt the drive to tell these stories. Not just ones about poverty but about potential too. I believed that people would respond very differently to a narrative focused on a story of entrepreneurship versus a narrative focused solely on need. I was curious to see if someone hearing that kind of narrative would feel motivated to help in a new way, by lending money to a capable entrepreneur directly instead of donating money to a nonprofit.

There are many underprivileged entrepreneurs I've met all around the world who make amazing things happen in their own lives.

Using her ears in East Africa

It was a super humbling experience. I realized that you can't just show up in a new country and start trying to be useful. It's counterproductive. At best, your first impressions are only scratching the surface of reality there. At worst, you risk misunderstandings thereby causing actual damage to a community you aim to help.

The more I have travelled and worked in other countries, the more I've learned not to make assumptions about someone else's life and experiences. The best decisions I've made have come from listening closely to the people I want to serve.

Individuals themselves will always know what is best for them and their families. It might make you feel good offering them a leftover t-shirt or inventory from your company, but that is not the best way to help. The best way to help is to listen with an open heart. Help by not holding any assumptions and preferences about cultures and people with which you're unfamiliar.

Rather than seeing people as needing endless handouts to survive, I've realized that many people are determined and resourceful if given the means.

Jessica's favorite Kiva story

I have several stories in my book, "Clay Water Brick: Finding Inspiration From Entrepreneurs Who Do the Most With the Least." I will share with you the story about when I met Patrick in Eastern Uganda.

As a boy, Patrick lost most of his family when a militant rebel group attacked his village. Patrick and his brother fled. After weeks of traveling, they settled in a village where they found distant cousins.

Imagine this. Patrick and his brother had no home, no food, no money, and not even shoes on their feet. They were young, orphaned, uneducated, homeless, and hungry.

After wondering if he would even be able to eat one morning, Patrick had an idea. He rolled up his sleeves and began to dig. He used a thick, short piece of wood and scraps of metal as tools. As he dug, he discovered that certain patches of rust-colored earth were harder, and contained more clay than others. He experimented and found that if he mixed the clay with water until it was the right consistency, it could be shaped. With his bare hands and a scrap of wood, he began to work the clay into bricks. It took him a while to get some bricks good enough to sell for a fraction of a penny each.

He saved money over time until he could afford a wooden brick mold that could help him make better bricks. Over time, he was able to slowly sell them for more money.

Patrick let his bricks dry in the sun, but he knew that they could be made stronger if they were fired. He saved money and bought matches, gathered kindling, and stacked bricks around it to create a self-contained kiln. These bricks sold for even more.

He eventually was able to afford a shovel, trowel, and charcoal versus wood for his fire. Soon he had enough work and money to hire his brother and then a neighbor. When I met Patrick in 2004, he had employed several people, had a thriving business, and had built a lovely new home for himself--out of his very own baked mud bricks.

Patrick found a way to dig into the earth. That was the moment he created a new life for himself. He saw opportunity where others saw none without an education or resources. He saw potential within himself, despite all that he faced. He found a way to do something.

In 2005, I co-founded Kiva, the world's first personal microlending platform. Through Kiva.org, individuals can lend as little as $25 at a time to people around the world in need of funding to start or grow a microenterprise. To date, Kiva has facilitated more than $1.3 billion in loans (as of 2018) since its founding.

Advice to those who just want to give up

There is always something you can do. Even if all you have is a smile, you can reach out and be kind to a person.

Discover what you want to build or accomplish, then just take one step. Then the next. And then the next. Don't get overwhelmed by the bigger goals you might have. One step at a time is the only way to get there.

How being creative can inspire others

Professor Howard Stevenson of the Harvard Business School once defined entrepreneurship as "the pursuit of opportunity without regard to resources currently controlled."

If I were to rewrite this definition, I would say it is "the pursuit of opportunity, regardless of the barriers that arise."

To Be Creative...

I would say is "the pursuit of opportunity, regardless of the barriers that arise."

These barriers can make a long list, especially the invisible ones, like your (lack of) job title, others' expectations of you, your current influence, mistakes you've made in the past, or anything else.

There will always be barriers that look too big to overcome. I think great entrepreneurs use their creativity to conquer obstacles. Usually, people get hung up on what they fear. They might have perfectly understandable reasons for not going forward, but there is always something you can do to move forward and face your challenges.

I think creativity comes in when figuring out how to solve a problem without all the pieces there. There is always going to be something that the world can tell you as to why you are not ready or not good enough, or why you are not qualified, but great entrepreneurs figure out a way to do it anyway.

> There is always going to be something that the world can tell you as to why you are not ready or not good enough, or why you are not qualified, but great entrepreneurs figure out a way to do it anyway.

When survival is at stake

This is often when you figure out how to be resourceful and resilient. Because if you don't, there are such immediate and severe consequences.

Thoughts on college

I teach at USC (University of Southern California). Many students ask, "Is college today still relevant?" I think it's worth it if college provides you a really special opportunity for deep thinking, personal growth, important relationships, and much else. If college is out of reach or does not feel like the right experience for you, then there are so many other incredible and valuable things you can learn in the real world.

For me, college was four years of introspection, self-reflection, and coming of age. It was a lot of figuring out who I was and what I wanted. I think that kind of experience can be a real gift to people who are embarking on their career journeys.

It is not a black and white answer. College can be a beautiful opportunity for people if they see it as such, and treat it with the respect it deserves.

The biggest mistake entrepreneurs make

Waiting to start is number one. You have to start, and see if it works. If it doesn't, you must fix it, modify it, and then keep moving forward. Don't just sit around waiting for the world's permission.

The choice to become more entrepreneurial does not have to be this dramatic thing where one quits a job and storms out, and the next day begins again with nothing.

At first, Kiva was a side project. I was in school and my co-founder was working full-time. After six months though, it became a full-time thing for us. Did we perfectly execute everything? No! But it was enough to get the ball rolling.

Imperfect implementation is better than sitting around and wondering if your idea will work.

Be open to feedback. In fact, be grateful for it even if it feels mean, hurts your ego and doesn't feel helpful in the moment. It's good to learn other people's perspectives on your company and be open to all forms of criticism.

Beliefs that helped shaped her outlook

I was zealous, always driven by a set of strong beliefs. I believed that the main goal of my life was to express love. Some people said my choices were courageous, but to me they were just straightforward. I hadn't thought about them in terms of risk, since I knew I had a calling to serve and help others.

My faith was huge for me. For better or worse, I never made career choices based on financial reward. I always wanted to decide based on what impact I could have.

I was also blessed with a ridiculously supportive family. I had such a strong foundation, and I could always come home to that strong home base. That foundation let me go to the farthest places on the planet and feel safe, confident, and connected. That love gave me a sort of obliviousness to the riskiness of my decisions, because I knew worst-case scenario was just starting over again with my family's support. I always felt it would all be okay.

My Mom, is an educator, and my Dad is an entrepreneur. That combination of curiosity, learning, and optimism helped form my values, to seek out the "what if's," and try out new things in the world to see what might happen.

Starting over

Later on in life around 2008, I left Kiva and got divorced from my co-founder. I hadn't believed in divorce, yet here I was marching through this process. Yet, through this difficult time, I discovered a huge piece of who I am today

I had to reinvent myself personally and professionally. It was a moment in which I realized I had a choice to make the best of this experience and redefine myself professionally, not just as this person who got to be a co-founder of Kiva but as someone who was an entrepreneur and wanted to do more things. I used this time starting over as a time to reset.

> I had to reinvent myself personally and professionally. It was a moment in which I realized I had a choice to make the best of this experience and redefine myself professionally.

Even though this was a painfully tough time, I am grateful for how things turned out. I am very grateful for what we built at Kiva, and what we continued to do with it. Yet now with this greater ambition in mind, I was able to create a new path and identity.

When one door closes, another one opens

After my divorce, I spent three months by myself in Mexico, living on the beach, crying some days, and surfing.

Soon after I returned, Stanford offered me case studies to work on, which gave me an excuse to travel the world. I visited thirteen different countries in one year, interviewing entrepreneurs and writing their stories. I wouldn't have discovered this if not for my grieving.

I told myself I was going to feel the depths of mourning. I would mourn my previous path and the person I was, yet also give myself plenty of space to proceed wholeheartedly toward my new goals. I felt like such a failure, but I knew that it was going to be okay. I would remember my foundation and return to that.

I hope describing the low points of my struggles can offer optimism to anyone reading who might be going through a similar type of loss. Be gentle on yourself. I'm almost 40 now, so I've had four decades to recognize life's ups and downs. My experiences have taught me things will continue to change, but ultimately will turn out as they were meant to. Honor patience and your own life journey.

Reflecting back

If I could go back, I'd tell myself, "It's all going to be okay, and better than you imagine right now."

Jessica Jackley

If we knew how hard it would have been to build Kiva before doing it, I probably would never have done it. I look back with fondness at my naive 20-year-old self. I loved not knowing what was going to happen. I didn't know a lot about the world, and what I was or wasn't qualified to do, and that turned out to be an asset. I wasn't limited by anything.

We should keep that kind of energy as we barrel through life.

What do you want your children to know about making a meaningful life

I want them to know that we are here to love each other, and this beautiful earth that we get to live on. The point of life is to express, and experience love and connection.

You've got to step up and do some hard things in order to love other people well—not just family, but others. I want them to work hard to figure out a way to help others. That's what your waking hours should be about. We need to do useful things to better the world.

Manifesting what you value

It's useful to check in with what we love and value. We recently sat and made a list of the top things that we value as a family on a vision board. It says:

"We are loving, kind, compassionate, and forgiving. We love God and we are peacemakers. We are adventurous, confident, faithful, loyal, respectful, truthful, and generous."

We are loving, kind, compassionate, and forgiving. We love God and we are peacemakers. We are adventurous, confident, faithful, loyal, respectful, truthful, and generous.

What it means to be an entrepreneur

Entrepreneurs are people who overcome obstacles. Don't put a lot of pressure on yourself to go be an entrepreneur. You don't have to go quit your day job and start a company. There are other ways to still be an entrepreneur. At first, try to work, live, and go through your days in a more entrepreneurial way. You can figure out ways to solve problems that help the lives of the people around you. Start small.

Best accomplishments

Doing a *Ted Talk* was unbelievable. I got to check a box off my bucket list that day. At the time, it was the most terrifying thing I had ever done, but it was so much fun.

My other great loves are my family and travel. I've been able to see so many places in the world and embark on many adventures. That is invaluable to me. In the past, I've talked about the currencies people prefer to get paid in, but my **currency is adventure**. Don't pay me; instead, let me travel places with the ones I love or, better yet, do both!

***

Jessica speaks about entrepreneurship to thousands of people each year at universities, businesses, conferences, and a myriad of other events to groups from around the world. She is an entrepreneur focused on financial inclusion, the sharing economy, and social justice.

Chapter 10

I Told People What to Think About Me and It Worked

An Interview with Adryenn Ashley, Social Media Influencer

Adryenn has been an entrepreneur her whole life

I grew up in the age where people didn't talk about domestic violence. Because my Mom suffered abuse herself, she raised me to never be a victim.

"You are always in control of your circumstances," she once told me. "If you don't like your circumstances, then change them."

My lifelong drive comes from not allowing victimhood to define me. My Mom encouraged me to never allow things that were not okay with me. Those lessons stuck with me throughout adulthood.

Growing up though, I was *not* okay with our poverty. I lived in Marin County, one of the richest parts of the country, and where it seemed like everyone else had money but us. Even though I couldn't accept it, I refused to victimize myself.

I happened to be really good at sewing so I saw it as a ticket. I would go to the local scrap bin, spend just two dollars on fabric, and end up creating all these great decorated headbands. I sold them to the dance shop for $12 apiece.

Not only did this activity help me make money, but it helped me realize something very early on. I can and will make money anywhere, without resorting to the streets. I am resilient, and I will figure it out.

> I am resilient, and I will figure it out.

Growing up on welfare among rich people

All of my friends received cars as presents for their 16th birthdays, but I had to get a job to buy my own. It was really hard because Mercedes, BMW's, Jaguars, and Porsches packed our high school parking lot--cars I would never be able to afford myself. I made it a little game.

I began cutting school to earn money. I got a job at a public hot tub. It was funny because at 16 years old, I was an assistant manager at a place where everybody walked around naked. I didn't let the nudity bother me. I worked my butt off, and saved up enough money to purchase my first car, a 1972 Toyota Corolla.

The power of reinvention

It's so hard to be in a position where other people have decided your "identity," especially when you know yourself to be different from that perception. That's how people get stuck. They feel like they can't get away from their personal branding and have no power to change it.

The way I got past this problem was taking myself out of a negative space. I got a fresh start by leaving high school. Nobody I knew from back home attended my college, which allowed me to become a different person. I told people what to think about me and it worked! I went from a nobody to Director of Publicity on the student council. I completely changed my life, my world, my brand, and everything else by leaving a bad situation.

People don't leave soon enough. Don't get trapped. Do what it takes to fix your life now.

What Adryenn Does Now

My official title is social media influencer, but I like to say it's like being a social media pimp. I have a big social media following and I leverage it, using my influence, access, and audience on behalf of my clients who are often celebrities.

My secret is to start global conversations that matter. I start speaking and get people talking back when I find something I am passionate about--and passion can spark a lot of great dialogue.

How to find your voice on social media

I have many shy clients. They don't want to show their personalities in the public forum. They're private people and simply want to talk about their business and what they do. Unfortunately, when you only talk business, there is no way for people to get to know you, like you, and trust you. These three elements are the key to becoming socially viral.

The trick is to find four personal things to be radically transparent about. "Find four things you like to discuss," I tell my clients. These can be food, football, singing, cats—whatever it is you are truly passionate about that isn't too personal where you'd feel deeply uncomfortable discussing it. Being on social media is all about being social and open. This is the best way for others to see you, get to know you, learn how you think, and discover who you are.

Our very public lives these days

Times have changed. You can't just fake it until you make it anymore. The Internet has made all of our lives so much more transparent. People can tell when you are lying. They may not understand why, but they can still tell you are lying.

If there is something you are hiding, you have no choice but to be upfront about it. If you are not comfortable being in the public eye, you've still got to find some way to authentically present yourself on social media.

I know a ton of people who have no social media presence, no website presence, nothing whatsoever. They have an email with limited access; only four people know of it, like their grandchildren. They don't show up anywhere online, and have zero interest in being online at all.

If you want to live your life this way you can. I choose not to; however, I like that I can talk with 110 million people around the world about relevant topics. Recently, I had a conversation on second-hand smoking effects, like when kids are exposed to it in closed cars. I am glad to report this conversation actually led to lots of people quitting! I call that a win. Was it painful? Yes. Were the death threats fun? No. But it led to positive change.

Being an entrepreneur today

There has never been a better time to be an entrepreneur. Everything you need to succeed is just a click away now. Back when I became an entrepreneur, if I wanted to create a professional video it might have cost me $50,000.

Not only is everything at your fingertips, it's instantaneous. Projects don't require five to ten weeks anymore to complete. They can be done in a weekend. There are even hackathons where people build apps in only 72 hours. Whatever it is you want to do, you can now do it quicker, better, and cheaper. There is no excuse to *not* try a new idea or business model.

> There has never been a better time to be an entrepreneur. Everything you need to succeed is just a click away now.

Our path in life

Everyone's life has meaning. We were put on this earth to do something special. Our mission is to uncover our purpose. To that end, I recently developed a program called, "Curing Unemployment Through Entrepreneurship." It's meant to inspire entrepreneurship as an alternative to joblessness.

We have an overwhelming number of people who have no jobs in this country. Soon, technology will take over much of the existing low-paying jobs. Robots will replace fast food workers.

Cashiers will become redundant as we transition to a cashless society.

Once we recognize jobs are going away, we need to find ways to compete and survive. We especially need to inspire young people to become entrepreneurs because these are the people contributing to the most job growth. We have discovered that just one entrepreneur can create 31 new jobs! These may not be all new hires in an entrepreneur's company. Instead, they come about as a result of other companies needing and using their services.

My idea arose as a result of the 2008 recession which left so many people unemployed. All of us can rise together through the power of interconnection. Everyone has a destiny and something to contribute to society at some level because we are all just one piece of a bigger, intricate universe.

Conversely, when you are *not* living up to your God-given gifts—when you are not even pursuing them, especially when you know you have them, you are not just cheating yourself. You are cheating the rest of the world. When you play too small, you do yourself a big disservice. It's not just yourself you let down. It's all the people whose lives you could have positively affected.

We owe it to ourselves to be more. Our existences overlap in such a way that no one ever lives in a vacuum alone. No

> Everyone has a destiny and something to contribute to society at some level because we are all just one piece of a bigger, intricate universe.

matter how hard the struggle seems to be to get out there, in the end it is always worth it.

View of education

I hated school. I did not enjoy it until I got to college. I actually began taking higher education courses when I was fourteen. At sixteen, I went full-time to Dominican University. I had taken my SAT and got a perfect score. When it comes to school, the fact is you really do get what you pay for. My courses were spectacular and that's when I began passionately learning.

Around this time, I also realized public education wasn't designed for people who think like me. Nor was it meant for people like my son, Jack. At 18-months-old, he turned to look at me and said, "Mommy, this parking lot is similar to the one in school," I was like, "Wow! Okay, Jack. What does 'similar' mean?"

He scrunched his eyes as if to say, "How can you *not* know what 'similar' means?" Right then, I knew life as I understood it was over. I knew I couldn't put this child into a traditional public school, so I didn't even try. I moved to the nearby town of Strawberry so he could attend the best school in the area. I even made sure I was within two blocks of the campus so they couldn't say I wasn't in the district. School was hard for him, though, because he has ADD. He was disruptive and talkative. Jack is the kind of boy who is argumentative if he thinks you are wrong.

His kindergarten teacher was a goddess, and in my eyes the most remarkable woman in the history of academia. She was so thoughtful and understanding. But first grade was hard because his teacher was awful and she did everything she could to exclude him for being different, like sending him to the principal's office right before they took the class photo so he wouldn't be in it.

Little snubs like that were brutal for me to watch as a parent. Seeing him get beat up and bullied every day reminded me of my own childhood. Pain like that touches you deep down into your soul. It makes you think, *"How can I do this to my child? How can I put my kid in this environment of abuse every day because they say I have to send him to school?"*

From my own personal experiences, I knew there had to be a better way. When I first brought up home-schooling to a good friend, she advised me not to. She said it would it would destroy my child. But as things continued to worsen, I decided I'd had enough. I hired a licensed teacher to personally educate Jack. It ended up costing less than private school and he was given the education of kings.

Nowadays, Jack pretty much home-schools himself. We use the public education program called K-12, which allows him to go at his own pace. It's amazing. Some days he is on a science kick, and he'll do ten science units in one day just because he likes it so much and is interested in what he's learning. My son doesn't do transitions well, so I don't make him. If he wants to do ten units of just one subject at a time, I encourage him to go for it.

Trying to fit everybody in one box, and then making them feel wrong for not fitting in, is like telling everyone they need to wear a size-seven shoe.

Overall, I find public education tries to put kids like him in a box. It doesn't consider their strengths. It focuses on weaknesses and punishes them so they can conform and be "better." Trying to fit everybody in one box, and then making them feel wrong for not fitting in, is like telling everyone they need to wear a size-seven shoe. If you don't fit into this shoe size, you are expected to either deal with it being too big or try to shove your foot in. It doesn't work.

Not every child learns the same way. Artsy children are not the same as science-oriented children. There are so many different learning styles but public school doesn't account for that. These schools are failing our kids. I wholeheartedly believe you should be able to choose whatever school is in the best interest of your child, no matter the geography or what the public standards say is right for your child. Find the solution that works in the best interest of your child.

The right people you need to build your best team

When building a team, the number one thing you need to look for is someone to do the things you can't. You want to make sure you have a team full of people to pick up the slack and support you in your weak areas or with tasks you don't have the time to do.

Ask yourself - what is the best use of your time? Look at it in terms of profit. For instance, paper filing is not the best use of time. It would be better for someone else to handle that so I can handle the things I excel in.

Other qualities you want are honesty, dependability, and creativity. Honesty matters because you need to trust that the other person is going to do what they say they will. Dependability goes hand-in-hand with the first characteristic. A person can be honest yet be a total flake, making them impossible to depend on. Finally, you need someone who is creative. These are people who can figure out how to solve problems without relying on you. They are the ones who will help you grow your business because you don't have to hover or do their work for them. When tasked with a goal, true creatives accomplish it on their own and meet deadlines because they also possess the first two qualities.

Adryenn's philosophy

I have an ethical code and a philosophy. My ethical code is that I don't do anything I wouldn't want to see on the cover of the *National Enquirer*. And my philosophy is simple. Find what makes you happy and pursue it every single day of your life.

What's great about the new generation

They are the video game generation, so they don't actually understand the concept of failure. From playing video games, this new generation knows there is always another chance, there is always another try. Failure is not permanent to them. Instead, it's more like: "Okay, that didn't work. Let me figure out why not and try it again." What they can teach us is to never roll over and die. Get back up and try again.

Chapter 11

I Don't Want to be Hired by Someone Else

An Interview with a Socially Conscious, 16-Year-Old CEO

What makes entrepreneur Michaela Reddick unique

I am 16 years old (at the time of this interview). I am a full-time college student and the Co-CEO of the eSports Amateur Competitive League (EACL).

Company belief in giving back

We have an eSports platform online with 20 gaming titles. We host eSports tournaments and give out the largest cash prize payout for amateur competitors. Fifty percent of our proceeds from these tournaments go to nonprofits.

The EACL chose video gaming as a platform for social change

Video gaming is something that people of all ages and backgrounds can do. We even envision a future in which young people can earn a scholarship from playing. We have set out to create a universal platform to achieve the most with our fundraising with the idea you can play from anywhere because it's online.

It's time to change our perceptions about video gaming

Video gaming is the same as any other type of gaming. It should deserve the same respect as other sports.

It's the same principle as traditional sports. When you play, you experience team camaraderie. You can also make some awesome connections that could lead to business opportunities later on. People just have to open their minds and warm up to the idea.

Precocious beginnings

Originally, I went to a regular public school. A few weeks into kindergarten my teacher decided she needed to move me to the more advanced class because I was finishing my work before everyone else. All my classmates would still be working but I'd have to sit there and wait. Basically, it became like daycare for me.

The same thing also occurred when they moved me to the first grade, so I skipped to second grade when I was just six years old. My parents and I later experimented with charter schools because we wanted to explore an alternative schooling option. We wanted something more flexible where I could move ahead in my coursework more easily, but once I started with a charter school, I skipped up from fourth to fifth grade.

We eventually just switched to homeschooling and I graduated from high school at the age of 15.

Opinion of the U.S. education system

It provides a foundation for people who can't do homeschooling but it doesn't allow for an individualized learning approach. Homeschooling may not be an option for everyone, but I feel like the traditional school system is too rigid. You can't move ahead easily. It's hard for a student to excel in something past what the school system says you should be doing at a certain age.

What Michaela thinks of a college education

College is more challenging than high school because a lot of the work you do isn't as clear-cut as it is in high school, where everything is planned out for you. When you get to college, the problems aren't as simple and cookie-cutter. They get messy. You have to learn to roll with the punches and manage your schedule really well. Attending college while running a business is a challenge as far as time management is concerned, so I have to stay organized. It helps me manage all the tasks I have to do.

Establish career goals at an earlier age

Your high school years are when your educational drive has to become serious. You need to know what you really want to do because it counts. At that point, everybody is watching.

But it's important to begin even earlier. We need to be talking to middle school students, asking them to define what success means to them now so that when they get to high school and say," I want to be a biologist" or "I want to be a veterinarian," they have a realistic idea of what it is going take to get there. By thinking about these things earlier, our youth can start making a real plan for action.

> By thinking about these things earlier, our youth can start making a real plan for action.

What life is like for a young CEO

Very busy! I have many events to attend and a lot of public speaking is required. I often network to meet with non-profit organizations and representatives, informing as many people as I can about our platform. It's tough to still keep up with my school schedule because sometimes I have events on the same days as my classes.

Biggest challenge as an entrepreneur

Scheduling! My schedule is really tough. I have jammed-packed weeks filled with a lot of classes, assignments, and business projects. Plus, I need to continually go to our events, ensuring we stay in contact with a lot of people, especially the non-profits. We want to assure them they will always have access to us.

Pressure leads to prosperity

I'm under pressure but it's good pressure. Great things come from challenging circumstances. I challenge myself a lot. I challenge myself at school. I challenge myself at work. That's why I am able to prosper.

To those naysayers who think Michaela is too young to be a CEO

I have the skills. Just let me show you. Let me prove to you I can do something before you cast your judgment. Age is not the most important factor in determining success.

What drives her entrepreneurship

I wanted to be a CEO because I wanted to learn how to run my own business and be independent. I don't want to be hired by someone else. I don't want to work toward somebody else's goals for the rest of my life.

I feel like it's more personally rewarding if you work toward something that you know is affecting a cause you care about. I have a social purpose and want my business to work for me and others.

> You must believe in the purpose of your business, and that it can bring a greater good to a lot of people.

Number one essential quality of an entrepreneur

Persistence. You need a lot of it. There are always people saying, "I'm not sure about your idea. I'm not sure if this is going to work for us; if this is realistic or not." To counter that, you must believe in the purpose of your business, and that it can bring a greater good to a lot of people.

Michaela's inner CEO circle

My team of influencers is my CEO circle which includes a group of like-minded college students who deeply care about the social causes we're helping through our fundraising platform. Together, we work closely with non-profits. I stay in contact with them so we can ensure our fundraising campaign goes smoothly. We are also actively recruiting other college students who want to work closely with non-profits, create fundraisers, and provide volunteer work.

> Stay organized because time management and prioritization is everything.

Who Michaela admires

Definitely my parents. They are the reason I was able to graduate from high school early. They are the reason why I'm in this business. They've always taught me you can be your own boss and make a difference that way. Other people I look up to include Mark Cuban and Oprah. They built their empires without doing things the conventional way. They didn't take the path everybody says you should. They set their own goals and prospered because of it.

Some advice from one young entrepreneur to another

Stay organized because time management and prioritization is everything. You want to make sure you get your tasks done on time. Don't get overwhelmed if it seems like some task is larger than you and too big for you to accomplish. If you set small goals and pace yourself, eventually, with persistence, you will be able to accomplish what you want.

You have to clearly define what success means to you. What is it you hope to get out of this? Once you know these answers, you will have more direction with what you're trying to achieve.

A generation of independent thinkers

I'm not the only one out there who thinks this way. My generation has a lot of people who try things earlier. They want to start right away and are trying to affect social change at younger and younger ages. I feel like the earlier you start, the more you control you'll have later. You will have had years of experience by the time you get to be an adult.

Overcoming early struggles

When I was in the eighth grade (this was before I ended up teaching myself algebra), I had a real issue with math. I wasn't good at all. I didn't want to touch it. I thought, "I'm just going to leave math alone because I am not going to need it."

My mother encouraged me. She said, "Don't give up. You are very talented in other areas. There's no reason why you can't catch up." I listened to her and went from a fourth-grade math comprehension to a mathematics major.

Advice for parents

Let your kids know what you feel passionate about in your community. Let them know how you feel because they might be the ones to affect change when it comes to something you care about.

What Michaela wants other young people to know

I want to be known for helping other college students understand that if you're passionate about something then you can start right now and make a change. Whether it's something in your community you feel is an injustice, or even something in your family that you feel you want to fix, you can start now and you don't have to wait.

Things are only going to improve if you start to work on them as early as possible. Go after everything you want as soon as you want it. Invest in yourself. Whatever it is you want to start, just start.

The benefits of older and younger generations collaborating

Experience is always good to combine with creativity. I would never tell a young person to stay away from collaborating with older people who have more experience because that experience mixed with a young person's creativity will foster innovation.

Some advice for aspiring entrepreneurs who don't have parental support

There is nothing more encouraging than having your own desire to create something. Keep surrounding yourself with positive people. If you are supportive of certain social causes, then keep researching in that area and keep studying. Constantly remind yourself what's important to you. Even if you don't have somebody else there to motivate you, you can motivate yourself.

> There is nothing more encouraging than having your own desire to create something.

What makes for a meaningful life

Life is meaningful to me when I get to help other people, and I feel like the best way I can do that is through my platform. We keep nonprofits funded so they can continue to do good in the community.

Chapter 12

The Human Race Can Do Better

Be Brave and Refuse to Accept Other People's Visions for Your Life

An Interview with Michael Ashley, Co-Author of Skip a Step;
Author, Screenwriter, Ghostwriter

 Lisa Caprelli and I spent endless hours interviewing people in this book who weren't content with the status quo and wanted to do something different with their lives. They, like me and maybe you, too, heard all our lives: *You can't do that. It's never been done. It will never happen.*

When I hear people say things like that now, I can't help but disagree. We can do a lot better, and the people we've interviewed in this book are proof of it. If you start with one person or a small group of people who believe something so strongly, they can do something about it.

The arc of the moral universe is long, but it bends toward justice.

– Martin Luther King

America has a middle class. We have a representative democracy. That's because our founding fathers, a small group of committed citizens, created change on a massive scale. They didn't do it without mistakes—however, they did something outstanding that we sometimes take for granted.

Michael Ashley   143

Whenever I see someone push against the tide, I think about what they did. Everything is possible.

We are now living in difficult, chaotic times. I think there is a tendency, especially among older generations, to think everything is going to hell; things are bad and only going to get worse. There's no shortage of dystopian movies and books to help push that message.

But in the upward march of humanity, things get better. For

"Never doubt that a small group of thoughtful, committed citizens can change the world. Indeed, it is the only thing that ever has."

– Margaret Mead

centuries, the slavery our founding fathers declined to address in the Constitution flourished in this country, and it took a century after it ended for African-Americans to gain any sort of civil rights. And yet, within my parent's lifetime, we've elected a black president. Things can change. Things can change for the better.

We decided to interview each other, the authors, because we learned so much at the end of Skip a Step's research.

With that said, I interviewed Michael Ashley my co-author. We had so much fun asking all these amazing and talented people so many questions.

• •

Lisa: What made you become a writer?

Michael: When I was ten, I fell in love with the Lord of the Rings trilogy. My parents were separated, and my mom's boyfriend used to tell my brother and I stories about hobbits, wizards, elves, and goblins when we went to sleep, and I loved it. I didn't realize until I was in fourth grade that the bedtime stories came from a book by Tolkien. As soon as I found out the books actually existed, I started reading them. The middle book—*The Two Towers*—I read in one night, I loved it so much.

Around the same time, my fourth-grade teacher, Mrs. Jaworski, gave us a writing assignment: write your own creative book. I, predictably, wrote about hobbits, wizards, elves, and goblins. When I turned it in, my teacher accused me of plagiarism: *"There is no way a little boy wrote this."*

My Mom defended me, because she had seen me write the story, so my teacher completely changed her tune. *"Wow! He's a really great writer!"*

From that point, Mrs. Jaworski began encouraging me. I started writing stories about myself and my friends. I was really into the movies, "Young Guns" and "Young Guns 2," so I wrote a lot of westerns. I also wrote some stories about my alter ego, Jim Turbulence.

A few years later, I had to change schools, and I went from being one of the popular kids to having no friends at all. So, at lunchtime, I would sneak off to the library and read on my own. *The Great Gatsby*, *On the Road*, all sorts of poetry, a lot of Ernest Hemingway. I knew by then I wanted to be a writer, and I hated school, so I hid the books I wanted to read inside my textbooks.

Lisa: *You actually did become a freelance writer.*

Michael: Yes. After detours through Political Science and Philosophy in the first couple of years in college, I landed in a creative playwriting class and got two of my plays performed at the University of Missouri. Even though they don't usually let J Minors work as reporters for the *Columbia Missourian*, I talked my way in.   Even though they don't usually let those students minoring in Journalism work as reporters for the *Columbia Missourian*, I talked my way in.

After that, I earned my MFA in Screenwriting at Chapman University. Upon graduating, I had to do a lot of hustling, paying my dues, and taking a lot of different kinds of writing jobs to build my name.

Lisa: *How do you feel writing can influence or change someone's perspective?*

Michael: The only real way to make a lasting change in people's actions is through their consciousness—through their hearts and minds—and I think the best way to do it is through the written word. There's something durable and long-lasting about words. We hear something, it's cheap; it's ephemeral. But when we *read something*, we tend to believe it.

For a long time, the powers that be tried to control people physically, but over time, they grew more sophisticated.

Nowadays, they know the best way to control people is through "hearts and minds." In other words, public relations or—propaganda.

> The only real way to make a lasting change in people's actions is through their consciousness—through their hearts and minds—and I think the best way to do it is through the written word. There's something durable and long-lasting about words.

Lisa: Why does writing matter?

Michael: Among other things, writing is crucial to distilling your message, into making the most concentrated and potent version of an idea. The act of writing crystallizes concepts, makes them more concrete. Jordan Peterson recently said, "The act of writing itself is a form of teaching, because by writing it out of yourself, you educate yourself." Putting your thoughts on a page forces you to direct your energies into understanding your subject matter.

Lisa: *Have you seen the writing you do—ghostwriting and helping others write their own books and stories— influence people as you described?*

Michael: Absolutely. There are so many examples! Rebranding, creating thought leaders, even just opening a view into someone else's life and struggles. Let me give you an example.

One of my clients is a Major League Baseball agent who tends to sign contracts with at-risk youth. He just came out with a memoir, because he wanted people to understand his background and why his work is so important. He personally survived a childhood bouncing around juvenile detention centers. He understands the lives of the people he represents, and that underpins his business decisions.

His book was a number #1 best-seller on Amazon. He was also on *Inside Edition*. He is getting his message out more broadly, effectively, and honestly—and with more perceived credibility.

Lisa: *Thanks to technology, audio and video seem far more prevalent than books. People don't go to the library like you and I did growing up. Do you feel writing is dead or dying?*

Michael: Writing will never go away. Stories are the way we understand the world. Going back to the times of Homer long ago, verbal stories were passed down. Once the printing press arrived on the scene, writing exploded. Then, obviously, the Internet.

Writing changes form. We may not be reading 1000-page books anymore, and we may be losing the capacity for long-form thought (which is a different problem), but writing is still everywhere, even in multimedia, and that is exciting. Terence

McKenna said, *"The way that we understand and shape reality all comes down to the words that we use."* It's not possible to communicate ideas without words. They are how we co-create the universe.

Lisa: Why do you feel people have a hard time writing? Why are so many people afraid of it?

Michael: Because it's hard to do. And it's made even harder when our educational system doesn't stress it enough. We've moved away from long-form thought. Critical thinking is like a muscle; if you don't exercise it, it dies. If you have never used that muscle, you don't have any strength in it at all.

Too many educators and parents make the mistake of not reiterating the relevance of reading books and writing long-form work. These are the best ways to grow your consciousness and build communication skills. One of the people I interviewed for this book, Dean Del Sesto, said (to paraphrase): *The best way to get ahead is to build communication skills.* To do that well, you need to read.

Another reason writing is hard is that it requires you to do one of the most difficult activities in life -- think deeply. We live in a culture valuing instant gratification, and writing requires reflection and thought. If everything is geared toward never being "bored," you don't have to sit with your own thoughts, and you're not building the skills underpinning good writing.

Lisa: If someone doesn't have time to read, but rather, they listen to audiobooks—do you think it exercises the muscles involved in communication?

Michael: It's better than nothing, but it requires a different level of concentration to listen to, comprehend, and remember an audiobook.

I think reading is the best thing you can do to get better at communication, even if you are not trying to be a writer. Take time to disengage from society for a moment, shut out the noise, and read something. No matter who you are, there must be something written somewhere that interests you.

> Reading is the best thing you can do to get better at communication, even if you are not trying to be a writer.

Lisa: What challenges and struggles have you faced in your life?

Michael: Stubbornness and rejection of authority. I didn't pay attention in school, starting from kindergarten, so I got bad grades. I never opened the textbooks, so I never learned what I was supposed to. What was important to me was being in my head, my own imagination.

By the time I reached junior high, I was popular, but that came with problems. "Cool" as I was in eighth grade, I started hanging out with high-school kids, driving around, going to parties. I lived a fast life for a few years. When I was fifteen, my Dad went out of town for a week, so we had a days-long party at his house. Then we took his car and crashed it. Of course, he found out, and when all was said and done, I was blamed for everything. Not just the party and the car, but all the trouble I'd caused the previous few years.

You know the phrase "grounded for life?" I was banned from going to all of my best friends' houses forever. For six months, I wasn't allowed to use the phone, watch TV, or go anywhere but home after school. And I still got in trouble after that! I was caught breaking curfew later, to go see a girl, and had to surrender myself to the police. Needless to say, I wasn't an easy kid to parent.

Lisa: *How did you change your life?*

Michael: Well, eventually, I got tired of being in trouble. I was tired of people thinking poorly of me; tired of feeling hated, getting bad grades, and feeling like I was on the outside of everything. So, in my sophomore year in high school, I threw myself back into my education.

I went back and relearned everything I had missed in elementary school and junior high. I studied all the time, night and day. I'm happy to say that by my junior year, I won Best All-Around Student and was invited to a special program called the Danforth National Leadership Award. I had completely turned my life around.

Lisa: *What advice do you have for someone who wants to make a difference in the world and stand out against the competition?*

Michael: First, don't be like everybody else. Most people will want you to fit into a box. You can't escape that. Instead of trying to avoid it, be brave and refuse to accept other people's visions for your life.

When I was in junior high, my school had us fill out questionnaires to tell what jobs we were best suited for. I say the hell with that. Don't let anyone make those decisions for you; don't even buy into the idea that you need to have a job. Who's to say that in 15 to 20 years, jobs will even exist?

Seth Godin says, *That time is past where that trade was reliable.* When you look at work in the 50's and 60's, people were essentially machines, but you could expect a pension, health benefits and basic security from your job. Those jobs don't exist anymore, so don't be a machine. Make your own path. Don't do what society expects from you. By forging your own path, you will find your own people—Godin calls them "Your Tribe"—the people who resonate with you.

Success may not happen right away. There will be moments when you feel completely isolated and alone, especially when you go against the grain. Over time, if you stick with it, bring value to your work, and treat people with kindness, you will develop that tribe of people who will keep you going.

Lisa: If you could talk to your younger self, what advice would you give him to "skip a step"? How do you give yourself shortcuts in life?

Michael: I burned too many bridges when I was younger. I spoke without thinking, and not always nicely. In retrospect, I would have saved time and heartbreak if I had known the best way to develop the right relationships. I could have learned that method from some of the people who I blew off.

If you're trying to break into a difficult field, like the entertainment industry, drop the idea that someone will come out of nowhere and recognize your genius. That does happen every so often, and it's wonderful when it does, but it isn't likely.

If you want to skip a step, to bypass the pipe dream of chance discovery, align yourself with centers of influence and power. Build your connections with those people, let them lecture you, let them show you what they did first.

Also, while you are learning from people, give back; make the relationships reciprocal. Make yourself useful and valuable, and when the time is right, push your own work. And truly, learn from my mistakes. Don't burn your bridges.

*Lisa: **What makes you cry?***

Michael: The passage of time, when I think about milestones. Recently, I took my three-year-old son to his classroom, and we were talking about dinosaurs and toys. I looked at him and could see that he will never again be the baby he was. I could see the future happening—he will go to school, have a career Everything is temporary, and it really got to me. Time only flows in one direction. Appreciate everything today because you are not coming back.

*Lisa: **I've been saying since I was little girl that writing is a legacy no one can take away. Do you feel that when your children are grown, and you pass from this earth, as we all do, they will be able to grasp your vision?***

Michael: Absolutely. That's what I've tried to do for a long time. I've had bad corporate jobs and felt like my potential was being squandered. I've felt purposeless and felt like I was cheating myself and others by not following my dreams. But now I am an entrepreneur—I'm following my dreams. Yes, some days are harder than others, but they're all still glorious and wonderful. On the bad days, I remind myself that I'm doing work that is meaningful. I make a difference.

*Lisa: **What do you feel is the meaning of life?***

Michael: Finding your value and discovering how it fits into the world. For a long time, I was a nihilist; I thought modern science basically reduced us to biological machines. You know, just neurons and protons. But as I've matured, I've changed my view. Our purpose is to find what makes life meaningful to each of us, and create the part we play.

Lisa: *What can young people teach us?*

Michael: The plasticity of thinking. Young people aren't yet beaten down; they aren't stuck in their ways. They are open-minded. They don't yet have mortgages, kids, and responsibilities. They are free-spirited, independent, and willing to try new things. They aren't stuck in the story the rest of us tell ourselves about "what has to be."

Lisa: *What is your why?*

Michael: The human race can do better. Our biggest struggle is disunity consciousness—people view each other as competition.

I'm not against competition, but we label people "the other," which allows wars and other tragedies, because we see other people as subhuman. It's why we are able to shoot people and hurt them; we can pretend they don't matter. Well, I disagree.

I didn't always feel this way, but I feel it now. I am one organism experiencing life individualistically, and my "why" is to help people sense the great connection between us all. I want to help people create art, find and create meaning, and help people come together.

I love storytelling. I see it as a way we can change the world.

I want to change our story, to make others recognize the value of each human being, every organism, animal, object, and tree.

Everyone and everything has purpose and meaning. And when we change the story that says otherwise, we can change ourselves and our place in the world.

Everyone and everything has purpose and meaning.

Chapter 13

Live a Good life. Live a Life You're Proud Of!

An Interview with Lisa Caprelli, Founder of Skip a Step;

Author of several books and brand: Unicorn Jazz;

Mentor for Teens Who Want to Become Authors

In Lisa's Own Words...

I believe it is important to leave a mark in this one lifetime of yours. Time is promised to no one. I often say, if I died tomorrow, I have left some pieces of work for someone to fill in the blank or take over. Here is to skipping some steps!

My inspiration behind co-writing *Skip a Step* was to accomplish several missions at one time. To me, *Skip a Step* means fast-forwarding your life, taking shortcuts, and seizing opportunities. It's

Lisa Caprelli   157 about making things go faster without waiting. Just because you grow up poor or lacking in some way does not mean you cannot be anything or anyone you wish to be.

When my son, Trey, was in first grade, I used to enjoy taking him to school early to watch him run off to play at the playground. As he ran off, eager for the day ahead, I witnessed him every day skipping off to school. I thought, "Now there is a happy boy. It is impossible to skip and not be happy," I proclaimed.

Skip a Step, to me, also means a lot of happiness learned from so many people and their experiences. I cannot tell you how grateful I am to hear story after story of one's journey into happiness. If I died tomorrow, I have left behind "Skip a Step," and watch out, this is just the beginning. More Skip a Step books are already in the making.

> I cannot tell you how grateful I am to hear story after story of one's journey into happiness.

Happiness is a destiny and a choice at any given time. Looking back at my life, I can recall how I grew up a shy girl with a huge quest for knowledge and education. I did not have the opportunities available today to many people—thanks largely to the internet. Through writing this book, I wanted to show everyone they can become anything they desire, just by taking advantage of what is right before their eyes. Especially by learning how to create new and better relationships to help others.

Today, digital natives grow up with the internet in their pocket. However, for people my age or older, we are digital immigrants. We had to learn how to use smartphones and the types of technology so many of us now take for granted. Importantly, even though the younger generation has access to all of this innovation, they don't have access to the stories and the experiences the older generations have been privy to. Stories are getting lost. Meaning is getting lost.

I truly believe if you have the ability as a parent, an older person, an experienced individual, or as a mentor, to help people change their lives—do it. This is the purpose behind *Skip a Step*—to share meaningful stories that can help others in their life quests.

I did an interview once and a question came up: "What made you who you are today. What did it take?"

One woman believed in me. Her name is Cindy Kirkland. She took me under her wing when I was in my early twenties. Back then, I was working at a court reporting firm in El Paso, Texas. She promoted me to director of marketing for her company and taught me so many things that made me who I am today. She taught me about communication, how a company operates, and how to think like a CEO.

What I learned from Cindy was priceless. I feel many experts in their field have a similar opportunity to teach and give back to the younger generation.

Skip a Step is so important because just reading this book can enable you to learn valuable lessons from exemplary individuals who did something great and were successful. Yes, the incredible people in this book experienced struggle, but each one fought through their challenges to achieve success.

Ultimately, *Skip a Step* is an effort to add value to people's lives of all ages. Now that is something worth living for!

***

And as we turn the table, Michael Ashley interviewed Lisa at the end of this Skip a Step book one journey!

Michael: *So, why do young people need a book like this nowadays?*

Lisa: Our book doesn't just ask successful people how they made their money. You and I purposely set out to ask meaningful questions of our experts—to go deeper. We even made some people cry.

Connection is so powerful, and we hope to connect with our readers in a meaningful way.

I want them to know. I want my children to know.

Michael: *This book is about interviewing entrepreneurs. You are an entrepreneur in your own right. Can you talk about your personal struggle for success?*

Lisa: Someone once told me, "Suffering is a choice." Suffering *is* a choice. I always knew I wasn't going to spend my time sad or angry about something that didn't go my way.

I moved to California from El Paso at the age of 29. Within a year and a half, I had partnered with someone who was in the mortgage business. I said to him, *"How would you like me to make you a millionaire?"*

And we did just that—and then some—in the years to come. We created a successful mortgage and real estate business. I earned my real estate license because I felt I had to know everything about the industry beyond just the marketing. I still have my real estate license to this day and I am proud that I learned something that seemed foreign at the time.

This business partner and I spent the early 2000's doing tons of radio advertising. We were on numerous radio stations. I used my writing and marketing background to write our own commercials. Our phones rang off the hook for new business. Sales is what it was about, and boy, did we get inundated with calls!

We built a brand and spent millions of dollars on radio advertising throughout these years. It worked, though, because our profits were way above our advertising costs. We grew fast. We worked incredibly long hours. I sometimes put in 12 or more hours per day, six to seven days per week.

Having my own company was a dream come true as an entrepreneur. It was especially rewarding as someone who grew up with nothing.

The truth is my Mom did an incredible job raising us, but we did not have any of the resources I found in California. Growing up, nobody in my family had their own business. I was the first entrepreneur in my family. Also, no one believed in my vision of moving to California. Therefore, seeing my first business become a success felt incredible.

Fast forward to the recession of 2008.

Anyone who lived through this crisis, especially those in the mortgage business, can remember how awful it felt when the economy crashed. I personally know what it's like to lose $90,000 in one month. I felt the darkness, the scariness, and uncertainty. Houses were foreclosed on, companies collapsed.

I exited my business, my partnership, and my marriage on January 1, 2009. After taking a hard look at my life, I knew deep inside I was unhappy and so did everyone around me. My relationship hadn't been going well for a long time and I knew it was time to start over.

Back then, I would plead to God. I would say, "I don't want to start over." Yet, in my heart I knew it was the only way. My problems were compounded by the fact I had a four-year-old boy and another son who just graduated high school. Nevertheless, I made the decision to change my life. I told myself, "You came here at the age 29 with nothing but one hundred dollars. You have a little bit more now. You will be okay so long as you believe in yourself."

Yes, I was scared, but I walked away and started over.

> "God, there's got to be a better way to find happiness and meaning!"

It wasn't easy. Before the crash, my husband and I were living "the life" on paper. We had exotic cars, including a Ferrari and a Viper. We owned real estate property in Palm Springs, Irvine, and Kauai. Yet, my friends felt fake. I sensed they only hung out with us because we had money.

My heart knew I was not living the life I was supposed to. I was living a lie. Something inside said, "You've got to change this, Lisa." I remember crawling up into a ball on my bathroom floor at the end of my marriage and crying, "God, there's got to be a better way to find happiness and meaning!"

Michael: *What lessons did your struggle teach you?*

Lisa: After starting over as an entrepreneur, today I can say I am successfully balancing "the Five Hats" of life, although it is a lifelong building and balancing process!

Hat 1: **Family**.

Creating a strong family legacy and dynamic.

Hat 2: **Friendships**.

Establishing meaningful friendships.

Hat 3: **Career**.

Thriving in business.

Hat 4: **Connection**.

Building intimacy and/or a romantic connection.

Hat 5: **Adventure**.

Experiencing challenging yet fun adventures.

Through studying human behavior my whole life, my interest in social psychology, and interviewing people, I now am writing the book **The 5 Hats** with co-author, Alexis Maron, MA, RDT. Without ever going through these life experiences, I would never have come up with this concept that many people love hearing about.

Michael: *How did you reinvent yourself in business after the crash of 2008?*

Lisa: Colleagues knew me as the girl who came here with one hundred dollars and started her life over in 2001. They also knew I made it my mission to put my soul into everything I did. Around 2010, I started asking people, "Can I market and brand you and your company?"

They responded so favorably. It gave me the confidence to launch a new endeavor; my own branding, marketing, and public relations agency.

Within a few years, I learned public relations inside and out, marketing companies in various industries, including technology, medicine, automotive, and more.

My efforts paid off so well that I had the privilege of becoming a professor of public relations campaign management at California State University, Long Beach.

Michael: *How has the experience of creating this book changed you?*

Lisa: In the course of cowriting *Skip a Step*, I've met so many talented and knowledgeable people in many fields. Interviewing numerous people, even outside of this book, because I love to study human behavior so much, has confirmed my hunch -- money is not everything. Money is not the key to success. It is all of it, as it works in your life and in the lives of the relationships around you: balancing the 5 hats of life.

Whatever is true for you, is true for YOU!

Younger people may think to themselves, 'If I have my own business, I will be able to make all this cash. I will be able to get all this stuff.' But the people we interviewed made it clear, all those dollars and all that stuff is not the meaning of life.

There is meaning beyond success and everybody defines success differently. For one person, success may mean attaining a million-dollar house overlooking the ocean. Another person may view success as achieving a strong personal relationship with their family. What writing this book has taught me is that I view success as finding a way to continually balance the five hats: family; career; business; connection/intimacy; and adventure.

Michael: *What's an interesting response to an interview question we received in the course of writing this book that stuck with you?*

Lisa: Michael Gerber, who is the oldest person we've interviewed had a great response to this question: "What is the meaning of life to you?" His answer was: "To create."

> "What is the meaning of life to you?" His answer was: "To create."

I agree with him. We started with an idea for this book just like every person who creates a business. The act of creation is so fulfilling.

Michael: *Throughout writing this book, we often asked, What can the younger generation teach the older generation. Let's reverse it. What can the older generation teach younger people?*

Lisa: My answer goes back to creation. As I said, a person begins a business by starting with an idea. Yet after several years, inertia creeps in. They lose that spark. They're now on auto-pilot. They are not in the mood to create anymore.

I see this all of the time with what I refer to as *business dinosaurs*. These are older people who don't bother to learn new technology. They don't get social media. They don't see the need for a digital presence, or how the changing cultural or technological landscape could help their company.

Well, this same older person who has successfully been in business for a long time could collaborate with younger people who are curious and knowledgeable about emerging technology.

The fact is these business dinosaurs are veterans in their field with experience and wisdom to share. If they were to team up with a younger, techn-savvy person fresh out of college they could be unstoppable. A real symbiotic relationship might take place with both generations benefitting from each other.

Michael: *What advice would you give a young person starting out in business?*

Lisa: Seek out a mentor. Don't be afraid to ask, volunteer, or help someone, especially in the field you aspire to work in. Give your time freely. If a teenager came to me and said, "Lisa I'd like to help you because I want to learn from you," I would be impressed. I would give them a chance.

When I see kids on the phone all the time playing with social media, I think to myself, "If I was their age I would figure out a way to either gain experience—which is priceless—or get paid doing the same thing so the whole world would open for me.

Michael: *We talked earlier about this, but let's dive deeper. This book is not just about succeeding financially. It's about living the best and most meaningful life. How do you define a meaningful life?*

Lisa: I want to leave a legacy. I want to keep writing as long as I can put meaningful or creative sentences together.

To say, "I'm happy now" sounds so cliché. But I *am* happy and you know what? I've gone through the struggle, the pain, and come out the other side. I'm blessed materially. My family is secure and I am in a loving relationship today. All my hats are fulfilled. That's happiness. That's a meaningful life.

There will always be problems. Your attitude is still a choice.

> For every 60 seconds of anger,
> you lose 60 seconds of happiness.
> For every 60 seconds of sadness,
> you lose 60 seconds of happiness.

My son recently said to me, "For every 60 seconds of anger, you lose 60 seconds of happiness. For every 60 seconds of sadness, you lose 60 seconds of happiness."

He hears me talk all the time about the meaning of life. He's also heard me say that when I die, "This baton is yours. You get to take over."

What that means is there's lots of work to be done in this world to make a difference. It might take a minute or it might take you ten years, but you have the choice to do the important work. It's up to you. And other young people like you. That's what *Skip a Step* is all about.

Michael: *How do you stay inspired?*

Lisa: I try to remind myself to constantly be grateful. It's important to identify three things you're grateful for. It's easy. Anyone can find at least three things.

I'm always grateful for my family. I'm appreciative for the great people that have helped me along the way and support all my ideas from vision to execution. I am grateful that I'm healthy and that I hopefully get to live a long life. And if I don't, I'm grateful for the incredible work I put into my life will have meaning. I hope to pass the baton for someone else to carry it forward.

Lisa Caprelli   167

Michael: *What is the number one mistake you see young people making today? What would you tell them to do differently?*

Lisa: The number one mistake I see young people making today has to do with time management. *Putting off their idea.* Too often, they say, "I'm too busy." But wait a minute. We all get the same 24 hours in a day.

I also see too many young people not appreciating the everyday things in life; not appreciating the simple treasures. Be thankful for the life you have.

Young people do not reach out for help enough. They don't seek out mentors. They're afraid the person will say no. They have these blocks in their head that are all wrong. Even if you ask someone for help and that person says, "No," then ask someone else.

I must have asked him 152 times to participate. I did not give up.

Chances are people will say "yes" to you. Throughout our interviews, we have met so many successful people who appealed to mentors that made them who they are today. They didn't accept no for an answer.

I'm one of those people that did not accept "no" either. I approached Mitch Free to be in our book. I must have asked him 152 times to participate. I did not give up. Although he was busy, Mitch flew from Atlanta to California to be in this book, because I really wanted his story of perseverance to help others.

Michael: *How do you see the world 10, 15, even 50 years from now? Are you hopeful for the future?*

Lisa: Yes! I'm very hopeful for the future and I believe the people who are the change makers of this world—the individuals who use technology to leverage their voice, or God-given talents, and those who team up with the right people—can make differences in the world.

This is all thanks to technology. Technology will continue to change businesses and everyday life. It's going to transform every aspect of the human experience for the better.

Michael: *We talked earlier about dealing with fear; how you knew you needed to leave your marriage and start over in business though you were scared. For anyone reading this book, how do you advise getting through fear?*

Lisa: I relate fear to struggle. I've known struggle for a good part of my life. I will never lose that sense of struggle and what that feels and looks like. Fear comes from a feeling of lacking, of insecurity. However, facing struggle and fear head on can be good things—they can be tools for motivation and growth.

I can recall giving a speech on this topic where a gentleman raised his hand. "What do you say to someone that doesn't want to change -- to a person who thinks they have it all figured out."

He was talking about himself. I looked at him and said, "Apparently, Sir, you have not had enough struggle."

Here was a person who didn't value struggle and problems. But as inspirational speaker, Tony Robbins, says "Your biggest problem is you think you shouldn't have them.

But problems are what make us grow. Problems are what sculpt your soul."

Michael: *What is your final message to the people reading this*

Make it big. Do it well, regardless of the deeds or cost it takes!

book?

Lisa: Don't just live a laissez-faire life. Live a good life. Live a life you're proud of.

As F. Scott Fitzgerald says:

"I hope you live a life you're proud of. I hope you live a life that's true. And if you're not, I hope you have the courage to start over again."

Believe in yourself. What you want is right before you. Go do it! Build a tribe or community, and make a difference in this one lifetime of yours. Make it big. Do it well, regardless of the deeds or cost it takes. You will be a better human being for developing your own unique talents and skills.

****

To be considered for a chapter story in our next book(s), CONTACT HappyLifestyleOnline on Instagram @HappyLifestyleOnline. We continuously seek worldwide leaders and stories of meaningful and purposeful entrepreneurs and professionals for blogs, articles, YouTube videos and more. Thank you so much for being a part of this important journey!

Below: Interview with Joe Garner

Above: Interview with Mitch Free by Lisa Caprelli | 2017

Above: Jessica Jackley with Trey Solomon (Lisa Caprelli's son) | 2016

Above: Joe Garner Interview, Monica Petruzzelli, Lisa, Michael, Zara Safdar

Above: With Ken Kerry

Below: Lisa, Michael, Monica Petruzzelli and Mark Shockley at his studio's set.

Lisa Caprelli

It's a wrap!

Acknowledgements:

Cindy Kirkland, Sandy Hanneman, Keyana Martinez, , Blake Pinto, Matthew Vasquez, Kerri Kasem, Zara Safdar, Monica Petruzelli, Ryan Hawke-East, Jasmine Powers, Debbie Powers, Mike Hernandez, Donna Hernandez, Stephen Christensen, Rebecca Koch, Joe Dorsey, Chris Herzig, Suzanne Price Verdult, Rg Lutz, Jesse Kove, Bill Gearhart, Guy Navarro, Ted Hankin, Jaidin Holder, Miguel Barillas, Phil Ehrlich, Teri Sawyer Tom Martin, and all of you who had a heart print in Skip a Step.

Other books by Happy Lifestyle Online:

Instagram.com/LisaCaprelli

Lisa Caprelli

177

Made in the USA
Lexington, KY
09 November 2019